SPIRIT-FILLED Anointed by Christ, The King

by

Jack Hayford

SPIRIT-FILLED: Anointed by Christ, The King

Unless otherwise noted, all Scripture references are from The New King James Version.
Copyright © 1979, 1980, 1982, by Thomas Nelson, Inc.
Nashville, Tennessee. All rights reserved.

International Standard Book Number 0-916847-04-7

Library of Congress Catalog Card Number 84-080747

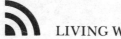 LIVING WAY MINISTRIES

Copyright © 1985 Jack Hayford
Published by Living Way Ministries
Van Nuys, CA 91405-2499

Table of Contents

SPIRIT-FILLED: Anointed by Christ, The King

Introduction

Little children ... you have an anointing from the Holy One, and ... the anointing which you have received from Him abides in you. ...

I John 2:18-27

To be SPIRIT-FILLED is to come to the King Himself — to bow at Jesus' feet and receive divine enablement from His own hand.

To be SPIRIT-FILLED is to experience Christ unselfishly sharing with you the *same* power for living and serving which He experienced Himself — the power of the Holy Spirit.

To be SPIRIT-FILLED is to have the Holy Spirit — the oil of heaven — poured out from God's Throne and into your own being; to be anointed by Christ the King.

There are *three reasons* Jesus Christ wants to anoint every redeemed son and daughter of God; *three abilities* He wants to enhance and expand in each of us; and *three offices* He wants us to fulfill.

The three *reasons* we must be anointed are:

—However sincere we may be, by our own energy we cannot *worship* God as freely and as fully as He deserves;

—However zealous we may be, in our own energy we cannot *witness* for Christ as effectively as He desires; and

—However capable we may be, with our own energy we cannot do *warfare* for Christ as penetratingly as He directs.

The three *abilities* Christ's anointing gives when a believer is Spirit-filled are:

—He *expands* our capacity for worshipping;

—He *extends* our dynamic for witnessing; and

—He *expels* the Adversary through our spiritual warfare.

Then there are three *offices* which involve our receiving an anointing.

At the heart of this marvelous plan the Lord Jesus Christ has arranged to insure our sufficiency for New Testament living is a beautiful Old Testament picture: the practice of anointing — of pouring holy oil upon candidates for holy offices, as a symbol of the Holy Spirit of God being effused upon them to energize and bless them for their task. There were three, and only three offices requiring anointing: priests, prophets and kings. Each presents an example from which we can learn, and prefigures a role which we are to fulfill. The Spirit-filled life of expanded worship (as priests), extended witness (as prophets) and expelling warfare (as kings) is no accidental parallel. The Holy Spirit has been given to anoint us to experience all God foresaw, designed and forecast from the beginning:

> *It shall come to pass in the last days, says God,*
> *I will pour out of my Spirit on all flesh;*
>
> Acts 2:17

Thus, as New Testament priests, we are *ennobled* to offer new dimensions of sacrifice in our worship to God Almighty, Creator of us all.

But you are a chosen generation, a royal priesthood,
a holy nation, His own special people, that you may
proclaim the praises of Him who called you out of
darkness into His marvelous light;

I Peter 2:9

As New Testament prophets, we are *enabled* to reach new dimensions of globe-girdling witness in the Name of Jesus of Nazareth, the Son of God.

But you shall receive power when the Holy Spirit has
come upon you; and you shall be witnesses to Me in
Jerusalem, and in all Judea and Samaria, and to the
end of the earth.

Acts 1:8

And as New Testament kings, we are *enriched* to rule at new dimensions of Kingdom authority and power through the ministry of the Holy Spirit.

. . . To Him who loved us and washed us from our
sins in His own blood, and has made us kings and
priests to His God and Father. . . .

Revelation 1:5, 6

The Spirit-filled life is the *new-dimensioned* life of worship, witness and warfare. And the key to its realization is the anointing Jesus places on your life — like heavenly oil poured over the head of priests, prophets and kings in ancient times. That anointing is the result of being *filled* with, *overflowed* by and *baptized* in the Holy Spirit.

This promised anointing is for everyone who has received Jesus as their Savior. And with so many new dimensions of practical, spiritual possibility flowing from that anointing, let's come to Christ Himself and allow Him to do that work in us all.

Let Him do it.

Let Jesus fill you with the Holy Spirit!

— *Jack W. Hayford*

SPIRIT-FILLED

Spirit-filled!
Let nothing but Your light
    shine through me, Lord.
Spirit-filled!
Now penetrate me with
    Your Spirit's Sword.
Spirit-filled!
Come, Jesus, now
    according to Your Word.
Spirit-filled!
Your promise shall no
    longer be ignored.

Spirit-filled!
As those at Pentecost
    in one accord.
Spirit-filled!
Dear Jesus, give me
    what I can't afford.
Spirit-filled!
Your free gift
    now upon me be outpoured.
Spirit-filled!
O Jesus, with these
    lips now be adored.

— J.W.H.

Chapter 1

The Promise and the Patterns

I magine your heart filled with God's love,
your mind filled with God's truth,
your soul filled with God's life, and
your body — the physical vessel of your being—
overflowing with God's goodness.

That's what the promise of "being filled with the Holy Spirit" affords us — the invitation to be filled with God.

Anyone who has tasted the love of God in Jesus Christ, who has been forgiven of their sin and been newborn into the family of God, has already found that the Lord is good. Now the call of Christ is to *become filled* with that goodness.

Becoming *"Spirit-filled"* is the third step on the path of obedience to God's call to each of us. Those three steps are outlined in the famous sermon the Apostle Peter preached on the day the Church was born — Pentecost. In Acts, chapter 2, the phenomenal things happening that day are recorded in specific detail. God's Word is careful to show us how He intends the Church to be, so the foundational patterns are important to our study.

Basic to our understanding is what occurred as Peter preached. People began to ask, "What should we do?" Their questions were provoked by what they had seen, heard and understood of the message and the events preceding it. Basically this is what had happened:

1. Jesus had left His disciples with the command to wait in Jerusalem until the Holy Spirit was given, and they had prayerfully obeyed.

2. On the Day of Pentecost (the day celebrating the Jewish beginning of harvest), the power of God's Spirit did come in mightiness, with dramatic, stirring signs of His coming.

3. All present were filled "with the Holy Spirit" and a miraculous phenomenon of speech occurred as Jesus had prophesied it would (Mark 16:17).

4. Attracted by and puzzled at this miracle of language, many attending the feast-day celebration asked, "What does this mean?" Peter rose to answer, explaining the whole occasion as a fulfillment of God's promise to fill all who love and serve Him with His Holy Spirit.

5. In explaining the miracle of those who had just been Spirit-filled, Peter goes on to proclaim Jesus Christ as Savior and King. He emphasizes that many of those hearing Him were guilty of joining in His crucifixion, and that since His resurrection now proved Jesus *is* the Son of God, they stood guilty before God Himself.

6. Thousands were cut to the heart as they stood naked in soul before this truth so miraculously verified in their midst. The testimony of Jesus' resurrection was somehow being mightily attested, both by the message Peter preached and by the miracle of speech they

heard lifting praise to God for His glorious works.

7. With that, many cried aloud: "What must we do?" Peter's answer outlined the three steps every seeker must take to enter into a growing walk with Jesus:

> *Repent, and let every one of you be baptized in the Name of Jesus Christ for the remission of sins; and you shall receive the gift of the Holy Spirit. For the promise is to you and to your children, and to all who are afar off, as many as the Lord our God will call.*
>
> Acts 2:38, 39

Here then, from the original statement and in the original setting which they were spoken, are the *three steps* to which God calls everyone who will answer His call and walk in His ways:

FIRST, Repent!
> Turning from sin to the Savior is the pathway of new birth. All who obey this step are NEWBORN (John 3:3).

SECOND, Be Baptized!
> Water Baptism is a command of Jesus Christ's (Matthew 28:18-19), and all who obey thereby declare Him as their Lord.

THIRD, Receive the Holy Spirit!
> This promised gift is available to each one of us in all successive generations since that day, as surely as the gift of forgiveness and the call to be baptized are.

It is important for us to see this simple fact as clearly as it is emphasized in the Bible. It is as though Peter anticipated that future generations may wonder if the same blessing, benefit and promise received by the Church at its birth would be available as time and distance changed. He not only stresses the availability of the Holy Spirit's fullness to those hearing him *that* day, but asserts that the same things being experienced on that day of beginnings would be timelessly available.

> *For the promise is unto you and to your children, and to all who are afar off, as many as the Lord our God shall call.*
>
> Acts 2:39

"To all who are afar off" is beautifully inclusive:
- —*racially* (for the Gentile world would be included too, in time);
- —*geographically* (for the whole world would be reached with time) and
- —*chronologically* (for though centuries would pass through time, the promise was made certain to all people in all places at all times!).

This booklet is about being Spirit-filled in the *same sense,* in the *same way,* for the *same purpose* and by the *same Holy Spirit* that filled those earliest disciples.

But it is more than about BEING Spirit-filled; it is about YOUR being Spirit-filled.

"For the promise is unto YOU!!"

What a promise! . . . *you* can be filled with God's Spirit just as Jesus intends *all* of His servants to be. To capture a sense of how fully available that promise is always fills earnest hearts with a passion to BE filled. So let the promise of God whet your appetite. Now that you've tasted the Lord and found Him good — now that since your new birth His Holy Spirit *dwells* in you — let's see how He can *fill* and *overflow* your life. The Holy Spirit — He Who has given that inner witness that Jesus is now your Savior, that you are God's own child — *He* wants you to take your next step and let Jesus *overflowingly* FILL you with His life, love and power. What Christ has introduced *by* His Spirit, He is ready to expand *with* His Spirit. The promise of Pentecost is yours for the receiving from Jesus' own hand, freely offered by God to those who obey Him (Acts 5:32).

Chapter 2

The Promise and the Passion

There is something of an urgency in the Scriptures surrounding the matter of being Spirit-filled. Jesus is urgent about it. Notice:

1. The night before He was crucified He spent a great deal of time teaching them of the "Comforter" (Helper) Who would come — the Holy Spirit (John, chapters 14-16).

2. Following His resurrection, He urges His disciples to have hearts prepared to receive the Holy Spirit's coming (John 20: 21, 22).

3. Just before He ascended to heaven, He made three pointed statements about His disciples receiving the Holy Spirit's infilling:

    a. *Its certainty: "you shall"*

        And being assembled together with them, He commanded them not to depart from

Jerusalem, but to wait for the Promise of the Father, "which," He said, "you have heard from Me; for John truly baptized with water, but you shall be baptized with the Holy Spirit not many days from now" (Acts 1:4, 5).

b. *Its priority: "tarry until"*

Behold, I send the promise of My Father upon you; but tarry in the city of Jerusalem until you are endued with (clothed by) power from on high (Luke 24:49).

c. *Its ability: "receive power"*

But you shall receive power when the Holy Spirit has come upon you; and you shall be witnesses to Me in Jerusalem and in all Judea and Samaria, and to the end of the earth (Acts 1:8).

Jesus' multiplied references to the need that His disciples be Spirit-filled make clear His concern that no one neglect this *third step* following (1) new birth and (2) baptism in water. He is pressing us past the human tendency to be comfortable with as little as possible. Since forgiveness of sins insures us of eternal life in heaven, and since water baptism indicates our willingness to become disciples under His authority and Lordship, how inclined we might be — and many have been — to simply stop there.

But the Spirit-filled life to which Christ calls us is one of divine fullness and ability to *spread* the love of God. He wants us to receive His power and touch the world around us as only He can by the might of His Spirit in us: ". . . Not by might nor by power, but by My Spirit, says the Lord . . ."! — a heavenly reminder that our best cannot begin to equal His almightiness (Zech. 4:6).

This same passion Jesus felt to see His disciples filled with the Holy Spirit is also seen in the urgent concern the early Church's leaders show. Two notable lessons are evident:

A. Samaria, 36 A.D.

Acts 8 gives the remarkable report of a sweeping revival which impacted the city of Samaria about six years after Pentecost. Phillip's mighty evangelistic ministry had led many to Christ, great deliverances had occurred and he had also led them into obedience to water baptism.

But when Peter and John came from Jerusalem to encourage and support Phillip, they indicate their concern that none of the converts have yet been filled with the Holy Spirit, "For as yet He had fallen upon none of them. They had only been baptized in the Name of the Lord Jesus" (Acts 8:16).

They were quick to extend that ministry to the new believers, recognizing the importance of that "third step." The Bible is clear that these of Samaria had been NEWBORN (they believed) and had received Water Baptism (see verse 12). Now, to move them along the New Testament way of discipleship, Peter and John

(1) prayed for them (v. 15),
(2) laid hands on them (v. 17a),
     and when they did, the Bible says
(3) "they received the Holy Spirit" (v. 17b).

Furthermore, their experience was neither a mere formality nor a casual exercise. Something significant enough occurred as they received the Holy Spirit that onlookers knew something dynamic had happened (v. 18). As at Pentecost when the first believers were filled with the Holy Spirit, people here in Samaria *knew it!* Any notion that so *filling* an experience would be less than unusual, should be laid aside. When He fills us with the Holy Spirit, Jesus Christ is doing something special, and we can welcome that prospect with peaceful confidence in the light of and with faith in the Word

16

of God.

B. Ephesus, 49 A.D.

Acts chapter 19 reports a similar situation. Just as Peter and John in Samaria, Paul comes to Ephesus and encounters disciples who, though believers, were not fully advised. Recognizing that, even though they had been baptized in water, something is still missing, he asks them, "Did you receive the Holy Spirit when you believed?" (v. 2). They answered that they had never even heard of that possibility. Though they clearly and truly love God, they seem not to be fully aware of who Jesus is. Paul calls them to be baptized again, in full recognition of all Jesus is and all He wants to do in those who believe in Him. As he does, he lays hands upon them — and ". . . the Holy Spirit came upon them, and they spoke with tongues and prophesied" (v. 6). It was a revisitation of Pentecost!

It is worthy to take notice of that passion which occupied the mind of Early Church leadership: every disciple needs to be Spirit-filled. Peter, John and Paul are case studies that verify two things:

(1) They were unsatisfied to see disciples stop short of Holy Spirit-fullness; and

(2) When people received the Holy Spirit, there was clear evidence of the Spirit at work.

They did not consider this experience either optional or mystical. Jesus had commanded it, so it wasn't to be taken casually; and the work of the Spirit was mightily evident — there was no mysticism, or guesswork about it. God was present, working purely and powerfully in the freshly Spirit-filled.

In each newcomer who received the promised Holy Spirit, we see in the Word a converging of divine grace. That explains why Jesus calls us too — to be filled with the Holy Spirit. *Hearing* Jesus' call to be Spirit-filled, and *seeing* the biblical evidence of a New Testament passion toward that promise, let's study the *purpose* for being Spirit-filled.

Chapter 3

The Purpose of the Promise

At the heart of the subject of the Spirit-filled life is Christ's purpose in our being filled. We are not discussing a passing moment of blessing or an experience to be realized and then shelved.

Entering into the fullness of the Holy Spirit is exactly that — an *entrance*. It is a beginning point intended by the Lord Jesus for our entering a partnership with Him; a partnership to extend and to minister His life, His love and His power to others.

This is dramatically illustrated in a figure of speech Jesus used: "He that believes in Me, as the Scripture has said, out of his inner being will flow rivers of living water" (John 7:38). His emphasis is on our *outward flow* — streams of life-giving water overflowing the inner man and emanating forth a refreshing to *others*. The force of this image of "rivers" is multiplied when held in contrast with an earlier figure of speech in the same Book.

In John 4, Jesus engages a very needy woman in conversation. He sees her sinning as the action of a longing, thirsty soul seeking satisfaction; so, in confronting her sin, He addresses her *thirst*. He gives His answer to every deep, human quest for everlasting fulfillment:

> . . . *Whoever drinks of the water that I shall give him will never thirst. But the water that I shall give him will become in him a fountain of water springing up into everlasting life.*
> John 4:14

His graphic word-picture depicts an inner *well,* a fountain to satisfy each person's *own* thirst. But then, as we have read in John 7, the picture of "rivers" is to serve the thirst of *others.*

The *first* is immediate, personal and internal.

The *second* is expansive, outflowing and extending.

The *first* is that thirst-satisfying provision of Christ as the Water of life, satisfying our sin-parched souls.

The *second* is of the Holy Spirit, like mighty streams of power flowing from God, surging from *within* the believer and gushing outward with the refreshing life of God, pouring forth from us to others in need.

The *first* figure is Jesus' gift of life *to* me and *in* me, answering my need.

The *second* is the Holy Spirit's power *through* me and *from* me, channeling Christ's life to answer human need around me.

The strategy was plain: Jesus Christ planned to fill all of His own with so much of His life and love that their overflow would continue to extend His power to all human need in the world. John explains conclusively that the "rivers" were to come after Pentecost:

> . . . *This He spoke concerning the Spirit, whom those believing in Him would receive; for the Holy Spirit was not yet given, because Jesus was not yet glorified.*
> John 7:39

So today, all who believe have a *well* of life within to answer our own thirst; but for Christ's highest purpose to be fulfilled, He promises an outbreak of "rivers" for the streaming of life through us and beyond us — to the world.

The Reason Above All

There are several scriptural and practical reasons why every believer in Jesus Christ needs to be Spirit-filled, but towering above them all is this one: THE POWER OF THE HOLY SPIRIT IS THE POWER BY WHICH JESUS CARRIED OUT HIS ENTIRE MINISTRY.

When Jesus came to John for baptism, He said that the experience he would receive there was essential to fulfill all God's righteous purpose for His life (Matthew 3:15). Immediately the Holy Spirit descended upon Him, and His preparation for the ministry set before Him was complete. We might well ask, "Did *Jesus* need special preparation for ministry? After all, He was *God!*" And, of course, that is true. Yet He Himself says, upon coming to John for baptism, "This is essential to fulfill all righteousness" (Matthew 3:15, JWH). Since He was sinless, the "righteousness" to which He refers is clearly not an act of repentance. Jesus instead is referring to that which would occur — and did — when He was baptized: the Holy Spirit came upon Him!

This is a simple but demanding point of understanding. Jesus Himself, though *born* of the Holy Spirit as the sinless and perfect Son of God (Luke 1:35), still needed another dimension of power for His ministry. In short, His perfection and purity were not of themselves sufficient for the task He faced. As God He was completely holy, but as a man He was completely helpless to accomplish His ministry. Unless . . .

. . . unless, as a man, He could draw upon the full resources of heaven's power.

The remarkable thing about this is how dramatically it reveals God's plan and unfolds His way for restoring fallen mankind. First, we must see how at His baptism Jesus is being displayed as the Father's provision for recovering humankind's double loss. Through sin, Adam not only lost his innocence before God and *relationship* with Him, but he also lost his God-given dominion for living his *rulership* in life. Thus, through Jesus' sinlessness the planned Savior is being revealed to establish for man a way back into *relationship* with God. ("This is My beloved Son, in whom I am well pleased," Matt. 3:17.) Then, in the descent of the Holy Spirit upon Him, we see God unfolding His plan for a way back to man's recovering of *rulership* as well.

Thus, in Christ, we have been given a dual resource:

(1) the *presence* of the Holy Spirit *within,* affirming our acceptance with God and assisting our growing relationship with Him; and

(2) the *power* of the Holy Spirit *filling* and overflowing us, to develop God's Kingdom authority in our lives and to extend that rule of love in our relating His life and power to others.

Here is His double gift: relationship and rulership; an enablement to know Him and to make Him known. And at Christ's baptism the fulfillment of "all" of this "righteousness" is a possibility available to us *because of the way Jesus fulfilled His ministry.*

Grasping the Implications

There is a joy-begetting reality to all of this. The Lord Jesus is wanting to place within each one of us exactly the same power, ability and resource for ministry which He had.

If Christ had fulfilled His ministry simply by the sheer power at His disposal as Second Person of the Godhead, it would, of course, have been wonderful to behold. But for us ordinary humans there would remain one awkward reality. When He would in turn call us to serve Him with dedication as disciples and with power to impact a world of need, He would be asking us to do something never before done on this planet. There would be no prototypes to view. We could review Jesus' life and ministry, but that wouldn't be quite the same, for He would have accomplished His mission by His power "as God," completely oblivious to any limitations of humankind.

But the Bible describes His having chosen another pathway:

> *Let this mind be in you which was also in Christ Jesus, who, being in the form of God, did not consider it robbery to be equal with God, but made Himself of no reputation, taking the form of a servant, and coming in the likeness of men. And being found in appearance as a man, He humbled Himself and became obedient to the point of death, even the death of the cross.*
>
> Philippians 2:5-8

The heart of a mammoth truth is in the words, "He made Himself of no reputation"; literally meaning Jesus emptied Himself of all His inherent powers as God. *All of His life was lived on human terms,* but carried out by divine power which He drew on with daily dependency the same way He calls us to do. He lived His human life just as any human being. Of course, He never sinned, for, being born of God, sin was never in Him and He never surrendered to it. But Jesus came to do more than live sinlessly: His goal being not only the saving of sinners, but the begetting of a new breed of men — a redeemed race. Besides living perfectly so as to become the perfect Savior fallen mankind needs, He also came to destroy all the works of the Devil, to break sin's power and overthrow Hell's dominion by sending onto the human scene a new "Body" of people — the Church — redeemed sons and daughters of God who would advance His mission of life, love, health and wholeness for all mankind.

> *. . . For this purpose the Son of God was manifested, that He might destroy the works of the devil. For whatever is born of God overcomes the world. . . . You are of God, little children, and have overcome them, because He who is in you is greater than he who is in the world.*
>
> I John 3:8; 5:4; 4:4

Jesus' mission to beget a new race as well as to recover a lost one, required a breakthrough in humanity's possibilities; not only making forgiveness possible, but *evidencing* the potential of *man's triumph in life.* By fulfilling His ministry *as a man,* daily drawing upon the Holy Spirit's power rather than utilizing His own special, personal powers as God, He presents us with conclusive evidence: victorious service to God is possible for redeemed Spirit-filled human beings. Christ has paved the way. He births us unto new life then brings us into new dominion. He provides His redeemed with the same power He depended upon and which He used in introducing God's love, mercy and healing to mankind, and in overthrowing Hell's strongholds.

This comparative chart summarizes it.

JESUS	HIS REDEEMED
Was born of the Holy Spirit Luke 1:35; Matt. 1:20	Are reborn by the Holy Spirit John 3:3-8; Rom. 8:11
Was sinlessly perfect II Cor. 5:21; Matt. 4:1-11	Are declared forgiven in Christ Acts 13:38, 39; Rom. 5:9; 8:1
Received the Holy Spirit's power for His ministry John 3:34, 35; Matt. 3:16	Are commanded to receive the Holy Spirit's power for service Acts 1:8; Luke 24:49
Triumphed over the Enemy and delivered the needy Acts 10:38; Luke 4:18-21	Are commissioned to the same ministry and victory Mk. 16:15-20; Matt. 28:18-20

It is clear that salvation's purpose is not just to make us heaven-ready. God's present purpose is to display Christ's love, power and wisdom to all creation (Ephesians 3:8-11). And that purpose begins to be realizable as believers receive the power of the Holy Spirit; the SAME power by which Jesus ministered as a servant and conquered as a King!

So in calling us to be Spirit-filled, Jesus Christ enters us into the realm of realizing God's fuller purpose:

1. He has given us eternal life, but for greater purposes than simply "being saved."

2. He will fill us with the Holy Spirit as a further step toward realizing His highest destiny for us.

3. By that means, He qualifies and commissions us to extend His life, love and power in the same power with which He ministered.

The grand purpose of our being Spirit-filled is to receive that promise God offers to all who will hear His heart; His desire for a people who will let Him be in them "Jesus Christ, the same yesterday, today and forever" (Hebrews 13:8).

In them his Son will be multiplied over and over again . . . And the world changed by His grace and power.

Chapter 4

The Person in the Promise

To be Spirit-filled is not to enter some mysterious relationship with God. There isn't anything abstract about it. When the Holy Spirit fills you it is fulfilling, to be sure. But it is important to underscore the difference between being filled with God's Holy Spirit and being filled with any other kind of spirit. Jesus emphasized this when He said:

> If a son asks for bread from any father among you, will he give him a stone? Or if he asks for a fish, will he give him a serpent instead of a fish? Or if he asks for an egg, will he offer him a scorpion? If you then, being evil, know how to give good gifts to your children, how much more will your heavenly Father give the Holy Spirit to those who ask Him!
>
> Luke 11:11-13

The clear promise of the Savior is that anyone who asks to be filled with the Holy Spirit isn't going to come up with something dry (stone), destructive (scorpion) or satanic (serpent). There are so many bizarre and fanatical things around, not to mention occult and demonic activities, that the Holy Spirit deserves to be seen in stark contrast. Let's see Him for Who He is, distinctly and beautifully different from the realm of darkness and confusion going under the general heading of "spirits."

FIRST, He is just like Jesus.

The Holy Spirit is just like Jesus, in fact, Jesus Himself said this. To help His disciples prepare for His departure and the Holy Spirit's coming, He said:

> *And I will pray the Father, and He will give you another Helper, that He may abide with you forever, even the Spirit of truth, whom the world cannot receive, because it neither sees Him nor knows Him; but you know Him, for He dwells with you and will be in you.*
> John 14:16-17

Notice first that in asserting the sameness of the Holy Spirit to Himself, Jesus says, "I will send 'another Helper.'" Thereby He affirms the obvious: He was here to "help" people. That aspect of Jesus' nature was already known, but now He promised "another Helper"; thereby saying in effect, "He'll help you just the same way I have."

Jesus further asserts the similarity between Himself and the Holy Spirit as He says, "You know Him for He dwells with you." In short, the Holy Spirit was so fully present in Jesus' own life and ministry that He tells His disciples, "He's no stranger to you. You've seen Him working in Me. Now He's going to do the same thing in you."

Of course, it is no surprise that the Holy Spirit would be just like Jesus, for He is *God the Spirit,* just as Jesus is *God the Son.* The grandeur of God's being is beyond us. The Bible teaches that He is so rich in His own being that a three-ness (a Trinity) exists in His whole self. Human imagination stretches to its limits in attempting to comprehend it. Yet if the universe, which in itself, though seemingly infinite in splendor, is but one creation of His, we ought not to be bewildered by the proposition that His Being transcends our full grasp. His Person is multiple within its unity: He is the ONE ETERNAL GOD, complete in the three-fold expression as Father, as Son and as Spirit.

Thus, our opening up to be filled with the Holy Spirit is essentially to be opened to

> The fullness of God's love in the way the
> Father has shown His love;
> The fullness of Christ's life, in the
> way the Son has brought us life, and
> The fullness of the Spirit's power, in the
> way His power is displayed in the Word.

TO BE SPIRIT-FILLED IS TO OPEN TO BEING FILLED WITH GOD. An old Gospel hymn expressed it this way:

> *"Filled with God, yes, filled with God.*
> *Pardoned and cleansed and filled with God.*
> *Filled with God, yes, filled with God.*
> *Emptied of self and filled with God."*

SECOND, He is our Teacher.

In the warmest sense of the Word, the Holy Spirit's personal ministry within us is like a Teacher: a patient, understanding, faithful Instructor and Guide. As a part of His introducing the forthcoming work of the Holy Spirit to His disciples, Jesus said:

> *But the Helper, the Holy Spirit, whom the Father will*
> *send in My name, He will teach you all things, and*
> *bring to your remembrance all things that I said to*
> *you.* John 14:26

As a Teacher, the Holy Spirit's help is not so much an academic process as an inwardly instructional one. He teaches us what to do and what to say at important times. He helps us keep our life — our conduct, our standards — in accordance with what Jesus wants and what the Bible says.

Since He is the one who gave the Scriptures, the Holy Spirit's indwelling will prompt or correct us in our thoughts or in points of behavior. We might even be inclined to violate the Word of God through ignorance or forgetfulness, but like a teacher saying, "Remember . . .," or "Do this," or "Don't do this," He will help those who will listen and learn. It may have to do with something you haven't even learned as yet, yet He'll correct before you fail. A good teacher will not sacrifice your future understanding by allowing you to violate rules at the present moment, even if you haven't advanced to the later stage. In other words, the Holy Spirit will keep you on track — becoming more like Jesus as you grow in the Word and in the will of God.

That's what Jesus meant when He further taught that the Holy Spirit would "guide you into all truth" (John 16:13). He helps us understand and keeps us consistent with the Father's heart and purpose. This requires listening to His inner promptings. An honest heart of integrity toward God is a treasure in His eyes. The Holy Spirit is a faithful Teacher but He is also easily grieved, and if rebuffed continually, He will *not* continually teach or correct. He only keeps teaching the Father's teachable sons and daughters.

And like a good Teacher, the Holy Spirit is faithful to prepare us for tests. If we heed His voice and obey His promptings, we can be ready for any trial or test, and we will not only survive, but we'll find victory afterward.

THIRD, He is our Helper.

But when the Helper comes . . . He will testify of Me.
And you also will bear witness. . . . .

John 15:26-27

The help the Holy Spirit gives is of two kinds —
assisting and dynamic.

1. Assisted by the Spirit.

The first is simply strength — strength in the inner
man (Eph. 3:16). Like a tree well-rooted and able to
withstand storms of adversity, the inner help of the
Spirit lends stamina and stability. The Greek word
translated "Helper" is *parakletos* — and means "called
beside." The idea is simply one of someone's facing a
job too big for one person, and calling someone to
come and help them. Imagine moving a table alone
and then having someone on the other side to help.
The ease and efficiency with which two complete the
task are without comparison.

And so it was that Jesus sent the Holy Spirit to help
the Church in the task of touching the world with
God's love. It isn't that we are *un*able to or *dis*abled
from serving or loving without the Holy Spirit. But
with His help an immeasurable, supernatural *enablement* is realized. He not only strengthens us within and
stabilizes us to withstand stormy circumstances, but He
moves through us in power, bearing witness to Jesus
Christ.

2. Dynamic in the Spirit.

"He shall testify of me," Jesus said, "and you also
will bear witness." The role of a witness is essentially to
provide *evidence for the case,* just as today a witness
attests to the truth of certain facts that are questioned
in court. This figure of speech — *witness* — is still
completely contemporary. Jesus is still standing trial in
the courtroom of a hostile world. The questions constantly face us, "What makes you think Jesus is *God?*"
"Who do you think you are claiming He is *alive?*"

"What nerve that you say He is the *only* Savior." The Early Church faced those questions with the verifying, authenticating dynamic of the Holy Spirit, and He is still prepared to bear witness to the truth of our testimony. When we bear witness to Christ, He will confirm the testimony we bring with signs that show Jesus is real.

The Book of Acts, rather than "the acts of the apostles," might well be called "the acts of the Holy Spirit." It contains the record of the young Church as it throbbed with the powerful enabling of the Holy Spirit as He fulfilled Jesus' prophecies: ". . . I will build My Church, and the gates of Hades shall not prevail against it" (Matthew 16:18). "And these signs will follow those who believe: In My Name they will cast out demons . . . they will lay hands on the sick, and they will recover" (Mark 16:17, 18). The record shows that the Holy Spirit not only came to help believers speak of Jesus, but His power testified to the reality that ". . . this Jesus, whom you crucified, (is) both Lord and Christ!" (Acts 2:36). The evidence was in: the Christ whose miracle power verified His Lordship during His own ministry (John 5:36; 3:2) was clearly still alive and working in miracle might and power. He is ready to do the same today.

The Spirit and the Word

Of course not everyone needs a miracle to verify the truth of Christ to their soul. Jesus acknowledged that some people believe simply because the written record of the Scriptures witnesses with power (John 5:36-47); and that isn't surprising either, since the Holy Spirit is the One who has given us God's Word (II Peter 1:19-21). No wonder God's Word is powerful and alive:

For the word of God is living and powerful, and sharper than any two-edged sword, piercing even to the division of soul and spirit, and of joints and marrow, and is a discerner of the thoughts and intents of the heart.   Hebrews 4:12

Yet as powerful as His Word is, God has used signs and wonders for its verification at times — unusual evidences testifying to the fact that Jesus is alive indeed. The Holy Spirit's power still works today, proving that Jesus has not changed; that He is the same today in every dimension of His ministry as during His lifetime, and as in the days of the Early Church — seen in the Book of Acts.

FOURTH, He is a Convincer.

Jesus said, ". . . It is to your advantage that I go away; for if I do not go away, the Helper will not come to you; but if I depart, I will send Him to you. And when He has come, He will convict the world of sin, and of righteousness, and of judgment: of sin, because they do not believe in Me; of righteousness, because I go to My Father and you see Me no more; of judgment, because the ruler of this world is judged."   John 16:7-11

It is in this ministry of the Holy Spirit that something of the awareness of His being God breaks through. That He attests to the Word of God and that He testifies to the fact of Jesus' Person and power by signs is all very well. But the convincing and convicting work He does is at the bottom line of His dynamic ministry: *He forces a decision.* No one can remain passive when the Holy Spirit is at work. He convinces people

(1) that sin is separating them from God;

(2) that Jesus is God, and that He is the focal point of all salvation; and,

(3) that this world system, engineered by Satan, is on a destruction course.

The Holy Spirit probes the hearts of mankind wherever believers invite His powerful working. He does what we could never do. He convinces people that God is right and man needs a Savior; that Jesus is that One Savior; and that eternal consequences are at stake. To more fully understand this work of the Spirit, we should notice two things:

1. *He is the One Who convicts and convinces.*

This is obvious in Jesus' words, but amazingly enough, even in the most sincere believer, a terrible human tendency exists to try and do this work *for* the Holy Spirit. Sometimes zealous Christians push the point of their witness until they become a contradiction to the love and graciousness of the Savior. There was never anything feisty or pushy about Jesus when He was reaching to the lost or the needy. It is one thing to feel passion and another thing to be pushy; and a confidence in the Holy Spirit's ministry *following* your witness will help keep that balance. Let's learn to do with the Holy Spirit what the widely advertised bus company asks its clients to do: "Leave the driving to us." If we try to "drive" too hard, we might easily drive people *away*. But if we simply and faithfully speak of Jesus' love and allow the Holy Spirit's power to minister through us, He will take over and *bring them to Christ*.

2. *He convicts and convinces INDIVIDUALS.*

The promise Jesus gave that the Holy Spirit would "convince the world of sin, of righteousness and of judgment" is not fulfilled on a generic basis. It doesn't happen all at once or to everyone at once. We all know many people who could care less about Christ; some who blaspheme His Name, others who mock or are totally indifferent to God's Word; and amid it all, how often it appears they do this with seeming immunity. There appears to be no lack of it, and often raises the question in us who seek to witness: "Is it doing any good at all?" But never let such responses discourage you or engender doubt. The power of the Holy Spirit is fully capable of breaking through *all* such hardness, indifference or doubt. Sensitive witnessing is the sowing of seed and with *watering,* it will inevitably spring forth as growing plants do through concrete. Prayer is that means of watering; the power that introduces and allows the cultivation of the Holy Spirit's ministry in such situations.

An early example of this "breakthrough" quality of the Holy Spirit's working is in Acts 4. The young Church was being bitterly resisted by the officials in Jerusalem, and pointedly told they were absolutely not to speak of Jesus anymore. The Bible describes their going to prayer:

> *And being let go, they went to their own companions and reported all that the chief priests and elders had said to them. So when they heard that, they raised their voice to God with one accord and said: "Lord, You are God, who made heaven and earth and the sea, and all that is in them, who by the mouth of Your servant David have said:*
>
>> *'Why did the nations rage, And the people plot vain things? The kings of the earth took their stand, And the rulers were gathered together against the Lord and against His Christ.'*
>
> *For truly against Your holy Servant Jesus, whom You anointed, both Herod and Pontius Pilate, with the Gentiles and the people of Israel, were gathered together to do whatever Your hand and Your purpose determined before to be done. Now, Lord, look on their threats, and grant to Your servants that with all boldness they may speak Your word, by stretching out Your hand to heal, and that signs and wonders may be done through the name of Your holy Servant Jesus." And when they had prayed, the place where they were assembled together was shaken; and they*

were all filled with the Holy Spirit, and they spoke the word of God with boldness. Acts 4:23-31

Notice how the Holy Spirit came in power upon them. And see how the message of Christ went forth with new force.

When the witness of Jesus is rejected or resisted, the pathway of power is the pathway of prayer. The ensuing chapters evidence an ongoing cycle of surgings by the Holy Spirit. He moves upon people of every station in life and brings hosts of them to the Lord Jesus. He — the same Holy Spirit — is still able to do as much and more to bring people to the Lord. Our role is not to attempt to convict them by our zeal, our arguments or our ability. The ability He has given is not to convict or convince — that's His work. Ours is to bear witness to Jesus Christ; then, pray for them, and let the Holy Spirit take over from there!

FIFTH, He is a Glorifier.

There is something especially beautiful about the Holy Spirit's commitment to exalt Jesus. In announcing the Spirit's coming, Jesus said, "He will glorify Me, for He will take of what is Mine and declare it to you. All things that the Father has are Mine. Therefore I said that He will take of Mine and declare it to you" (John 16:14, 15).

There is probably no greater evidence of the Holy Spirit's presence than this: if the Holy Spirit is at work,

Jesus will be praised;

Jesus will be honored;

Jesus will be worshipped as God's Son;

Jesus will be announced as Lord and King!

The reason for such praise, worship, honor and exaltation, as people allow the Holy Spirit to fill their lives, is that He — the Spirit — *makes Jesus real.* "He will take of Mine and show it to you." In other words, the

Holy Spirit makes Jesus more than a doctrine and more than a memory — He draws our hearts into His presence, to capture an ever-deepening sense of Who He is and how wonderful He is.

This is one absolute test of whether a place or a people or an experience is of God. If there is a genuine commitment to honor the Lord Jesus, to obey the Lord Jesus, to praise the Lord Jesus and to worship and glorify the Lord Jesus, then the Holy Spirit is truly present. One thing is certain, Satan is not going to glorify the Son of God. And as for the flesh, it will inevitably find a way to glorify itself. So expect the work of the Holy Spirit in your life to bring you into new dimensions of loving, serving, obeying, worshipping, honoring and glorifying the Lord Jesus Christ! And when you are looking for a place to assemble and fellowship with the people of the Lord, the hallmark of location where you can be confident of spiritual health is where the Lord Jesus Christ is praised and worshipped. In such a place the Holy Spirit will always be given the opportunity to work, the Word of God will regularly be taught and the glory of the Lord will be in evidence.

The Holy Spirit's ministry of making Jesus real — glorifying Him — is His highest desire. And when His purposes are fulfilled in this facet of His ministry, you will welcome the Lord Jesus Christ's fullest working in your heart, and you will want to worship and adore Him all the more.

Chapter 5

Partaking of the Promise

It was a Sunday morning during my senior year of high school, and as on any Sunday, I was attending my home church — a strong, evangelical congregation in Oakland, California. The message of the morning, being brought by a visiting speaker, elaborated the need we all have for increased spiritual power, and he spoke of the promised blessing of "power from on high" which Jesus guarantees.

He concluded the sermon calling for every believer to "be filled with the Holy Spirit," and then asked us all to bow in prayer.

The crucial moment had come.

To that point I had heard the truth with an open heart, but now I was faced with a specific decision: *"Do YOU want to receive the fullness of the Holy Spirit?"*

Suddenly, the most peculiar combination of feelings seized me. I could not explain why it was that I felt *both* — a deep *hunger* for God and a nagging *fear* of responding to that hunger. Why was it that I should feel such a love for Christ and such a desire to do His will, and yet at the same time feel as though a drag-line were attached to my soul?

It would be years until I would come to understand that syndrome of hesitation. But now, after teaching and preaching for decades and seeing thousands come into the fullness of God's Holy Spirit, I clearly realize how much Satan hates to see people filled. He fears the fact that with every believer who is filled with the life and energy that made Jesus' ministry so effective, his dark rule on this planet is increasingly being threatened and his plans for destroying eternal souls overthrown. And so, when any child of God begins to hunger for more of the power of God, with subtlety and stealth the Liar often comes to discourage, to create doubt and to somehow attempt to chill the soul with undefinable fears.

But that Sunday morning, notwithstanding my fears, I responded to the invitation. Making my way to the prayer room, I knelt down in simple openness to the Lord Jesus; the Christ Who had become my Savior six years earlier. And it was there, without pomp, but with very clear understanding and a real sense of encounter, that I received the fullness of the Holy Spirit.

Now, in addressing you through these pages, we have come to the same place; to the point that we have talked enough *about* the promise of the Holy Spirit: now, dear reader, the invitation is for you to partake of the promise yourself.

The desirability of being Spirit-filled is so very clear, I am sure you must feel that already. Furthermore, when all of that has been said, it is perfectly appropriate and timely that you *now* come to Jesus; that you now ask the One Who *fills* with the Holy Spirit, to fill *you:*

1. *He commands you to be filled.*

   "Receive the Holy Spirit," Jesus says; ". . . until you are endued with power from on high," and ". . . you shall receive power . . . and you shall be witnesses unto me."   John 20:22; Luke 24:49; Acts 1:8

Why would Jesus need to "command" us to receive a *gift*? The answer seems obvious: He knew fear would try to create questions . . . hesitancy. So, His command resolves the question: Come now! Receive!

2. *He wills miracles through you.*

   . . . The works that I do he will do also; and greater works than these he will do because I go to My Father.   John 14:12

Miracles do not require you to become "strange," nor do they substitute for maturing in Christ. But when the Holy Spirit fills you, He makes them *timely* and *normal* — given in God's timing and ministered in His spirit of love.

3. *This is the gateway to the Gifts.*

   . . . He will take of what is Mine and declare it to you.   John 16:14

Among the many things He did, Jesus was notably involved in healing and delivering people as He spoke with a loving and holy grace and power. Today, the gifts of the Spirit are that means by which the Holy Spirit advances that work of Christ. He distributes *those same workings* of Jesus to and through the members of Christ's Body — His Church (I Corinthians 12:7-13).

How to Receive the
Fullness of the Holy Spirit

Everyone who thirsts for Christ's deeper, fuller work in their lives asks that question. And it has been my personal feeling that to presume to tell someone "exactly how" to be filled is to risk substituting a formula for what Jesus wants to do Himself. He is both ready and able to satisfy your quest without help from anyone else. So in the light of all I've said, my simple encouragement to you now is, "Go directly to Him. Bow before Him. Open to Him. Trust Him. And ask Jesus to fill you with the Holy Spirit."

There are several thoughts — words I have often used to help counsel any who feel hesitant, fearful or needful of further instruction. But before I share those, could I rather *first* invite you to *pray?*

Your own words are sufficient. But if you might be assisted by the prayer I offer here, then make it your own. However you pray, the way to be filled *now* is to

Come thirsty and believing; for the thirsty will *be filled and the promise* is yours;

Matt. 5:6; Acts 2:39

and

Come to JESUS – for He's the Baptizer and He wants *to fill you*.

John 1:33

A Prayer

Dear Lord Jesus,

I thank You and praise You for Your great love
    and faithfulness to me.

My heart is filled with joy whenever I think of
    the great gift of salvation You have so freely
        given to me, and I humbly glorify You,
        Lord Jesus;
    for You have forgiven me all my sins
        and brought me to the Father.

Now I come in obedience to Your call.
I want to receive
    the fullness of the Holy Spirit.
I do not come because I am worthy myself,
    but because You have invited me to come.

    Because You have washed me from my
    sins,
        I thank You that You have made the
        vessel
    of my life a worthy one to be filled
        with the Holy Spirit of God.

I want to be overflowed with Your life,
    Your love and Your power, Lord Jesus.
I want to show forth Your grace,
    Your Words,
        Your goodness and
          Your gifts
    to everyone I can.

And so with simple, childlike faith, I ask You, Lord,
    Fill me with the Holy Spirit.
        I open all of myself to You,
          to receive all of Yourself in me.

I love you, Lord, and I lift my voice in praise to You.

I welcome Your might and Your miracles
    to be manifest in me —
        for Your glory
          and unto Your praise.

I don't tell people to say "Amen" at the end of *this* prayer, because after inviting Jesus to fill you, it is good to begin to praise Him in faith. Praisefully worship Jesus, and simply allow the Holy Spirit to help you do so. He will manifest Himself in a Christ-glorifying way, and you can ask Him to enrich this moment by causing you to *know* the presence and power of the Lord Jesus. Don't hesitate to expect the same things in your experience as occurred to people in the Bible. The spirit of praise is an appropriate way to express that expectation, and to make Jesus your focus, worship as you praise. Glorify Him and leave the rest to the Holy Spirit.

Stepping Into a Miracle

Over years of ministry, I have found this comparative study of Peter's experience of walking on the water a striking parallel to the step of faith being taken by believers who want to enter the walk of the Spirit-filled.

> *Immediately Jesus made His disciples get into the boat and go before Him to the other side, while He sent the multitudes away. And when He had sent the multitudes away, He went up on a mountain by Himself to pray. And when evening had come, He was alone there. But the boat was now in the middle of the sea, tossed by the waves, for the wind was contrary. Now in the fourth watch of the night Jesus went to them, walking on the sea. And when the disciples saw Him walking on the sea, they were troubled, saying, "It is a ghost!" And they cried out for fear. But immediately Jesus spoke to them, saying, "Be of good cheer! It is I; do not be afraid." And Peter answered Him and said, "Lord, if it is You, command me to come to You on the water." So He said, "Come." And when Peter had come down out of the boat, he walked on the water to go to Jesus. But when he saw that the wind was boisterous, he was*

afraid; and beginning to sink he cried out, saying, "Lord, save me!" And immediately Jesus stretched out His hand and caught him, and said to him, "O you of little faith, why did you doubt?" And when they got into the boat, the wind ceased. Then those who were in the boat came and worshipped Him saying, "Truly You are the Son of God."

Matt. 14:22-33

An Introduction:

Receiving the fullness of the Holy Spirit is very much the same as answering a call to walk on the water; that is, to begin to walk in the arena of the miraculous. I emphasize this "miracle dimension" of life, not because I believe we should seek the miraculous for the sake of sensation, but because we should expect the Spirit-filled life to have the same qualities that characterized the Early Church's experience of Spirit-fullness.

When believers receive the Holy Spirit on the occasions the Bible describes, special things always happen:

people lift their voices in praise (worship);

people speak forth God's word (prophesy);

evidence of God's presence is unusually manifest (signs);

miracles take place (wonders).

It is understandable that some people fear being thought fanatical to expect such biblical manifestations, for enough isolated episodes of folly exist to provide stimulus to those fears. But it is also understandable why many not only are unafraid, but boldly expect such present-day evidence of the Holy Spirit's fullness to occur. After all, if the One Who distributes the Gifts (the Holy Spirit Himself) is the One the Lord Jesus is pouring in fullness over the life of the prayerful, praising believer, then it is altogether reasonable to expect signs of His presence and givingness!

STEP ONE: *"Go to the other side"* (v. 22).

Peter's "miracle day" began by simply obeying Jesus' command to get in the ship and head across the lake. `

The beginning for any of us seeking to be filled with the Spirit *today* — that is, this *very* day — is to obey the Lord Jesus. Be certain no known points of disobedience are being secretly sheltered from His open gaze and dealing.

> *Examples:* Have you been baptized in water? Have you confessed any heretofore reserved, secret sins? Are there any people you need to forgive? Are there any reparations for past sins which can and should be made? Is there any condemnation you carry that needs to be laid to rest under the Blood of Jesus?

You may not be able to take care of all of these matters in one day, but the will to do so can be made in a commitment before the Lord Jesus *now*. Then, proceed expectantly. You are moving "toward the other side" in obedience.

STEP TWO: *"Be of good cheer! It is I"* (v. 27).

The tossing storm waters and the man walking toward him over those waves presented Peter with a frightening setting. In his uncertainty, he even mistakes the Lord he knows so well for a ghost (see v. 25, 26). But with Jesus' words of comfort, "It's Me," the complexion of everything changes. When he was sure it was *Jesus* approaching and not some other spirit, he was prepared for the miracle to follow.

Similarly, there are raging waters of controversy stirred by some today on the subject of Spirit-fullness. As with Peter, they often distract from our seeing that in the midst of it all, *Jesus* is coming to invite us to walk with Him in a miracle. Once the understanding is settled — "This is *all* about *HIM,* and *His* will for *me*" — the peace of God makes room for receptive faith to operate simply and fulfillingly.

STEP THREE: *"Since it's You, Lord, bid me come"* (v. 28).

Peter's confidence to answer Jesus' invitation to come, to walk with Him in a miracle, is established on the grounds that he knew *Him*. When Jesus says, "Come," the responding action was born of a *relationship* not a foolish presumption.

The same is true today with you and me.

The desire of walking with Jesus Christ in a "miracle walk" may sound to someone as though we are presuming to seek that walk for either self-glorifying or sensational reasons. But freedom to expect a new "miracle work" and respond accordingly is rooted in the understanding that Jesus is both the Giver and the Goal of that walk. It is *upon* Him we focus and *unto* Him we seek to see all glory given. Seeking to receive the fullness of the Holy Spirit is *not* a quest for selfish gratification. It is a desire to walk with Christ at a dimension of life to which *He* calls. No less!

STEP FOUR: *"And Jesus said,* 'Come!' " (v. 29).

Peter walked on the water! It's startling enough simply that *Jesus* did this, but that an ordinary human being did the same is overwhelming. We aren't overlooking that Peter later feared, doubted and sank. But never miss the doubly marvelous fact: he was rescued and restored! Peter walked on the water *twice!!*

I know of no passage of Scripture that more closely parallels the desire of the Lord Jesus Christ to welcome us into full partnership with His power and purpose. He invites us to "Come!"

So, do that!

Come and receive the fullness of the Holy Spirit, and let Him usher you into a miracle walk at a new dimension of power and living. This experience will not guarantee your perfection any more than it did Peter's. But in the same way that Peter survived, by calling upon the Lord, we can count on Jesus keeping us. He'll sustain you in your new walk with Him as you receive the Holy Spirit in fullness.

Come and walk with Jesus in a miracle!

Chapter 6

The Pathway in the Promise

Receiving the fullness of the Holy Spirit is not a climax: it is a commencement. The Bible record makes that point from the beginning: "And they were all filled with the Holy Spirit, and they *began* ..." (Acts 2:4). From that start, a broad development of "beginnings" follow, spanning the range from their experience of miraculously enabled praisings to their enduring of fierce persecution and martyrdom.

If the Bible teaches us anything about this miracle dimension of life in the Spirit, it shows it as one of adventure and adversity. Because it is a qualifying experience for moving into arenas of spiritual conquest, one can be sure there will not only be joyous blessing, but we can expect distinct seasons of struggle, of confrontation with evil and of spiritual warfare. There is no such thing as victory without battle, and the prospect of facing this facet of Holy Spirit-fullness should discourage no one:

First,	because you are equipped for triumph. Although the battle may seem heated at points, victory is certain in Christ;
Second,	because battles are *not* continuous. There are seasons of reprieve, of rest and of joy untainted by present conflicts;
Third,	because Jesus walked this way before you. He has blazed the trail ahead, marked out the dangers, and by His guidance you can avoid the pitfalls and walk with confidence.

Once you are Spirit-filled, you will want to take a very close look at the roadmap ahead. There is a pathway of practical follow-through provided us in the account of Jesus' experience after He was filled with the Spirit.

Then Jesus was led up by the Spirit unto the wilderness to be tempted by the devil. And when He fasted forty days and forty nights, afterward He was hungry. Now when the tempter came to Him, he said, "If you are the Son of God, command that these stones become bread." But He answered and said, "It is written, 'Man shall not live by bread alone, but by every word that proceeds from the mouth of God.'" Then the devil took Him up into the holy city, set Him on the pinnacle of the temple, and said to Him, "If You are the Son of God, throw Yourself down. For it is written: 'He shall give His angels charge concerning you,' and, 'In their hands they shall bear you up, lest you dash your foot against a stone.'" Jesus said to him, "It is written again, 'You shall not tempt the Lord your God.'" Again, the devil took Him up on an exceedingly high mountain, and showed Him all the kingdoms of the world and their glory. And he said to Him, "All these things I will give You if You

*will fall down and worship me." Then Jesus said to
him, "Away with you, Satan! For it is written, 'You
shall worship the Lord your God, and Him only you
shall serve.' " Then the devil left Him, and behold,
angels came and ministered to Him.*

Matt. 4:1-11

This passage gives five clear guidelines concerning
a person's walk in the new dimension of Spirit-fullness.
Seeing Jesus in the days immediately following the
Holy Spirit's coming upon Him for ministry, we can
learn:

*ONE: Don't be surprised if the Adversary attacks you right
away.*

There are many people who suppose if you are "led
of the Spirit" you will never experience trial. Beware of
such euphoric notions! The experience of the Lord
Jesus was one of *immediate* conflict with the Devil, and it
is very specifically clear that it was the Holy Spirit who
led Him into that confrontation. Do you think your
experience will be any different?

To the contrary, Peter says, "Beloved, do not think
it strange concerning the fiery trial which is to try you,
as though some strange thing happened to you; . . ."
"Be sober, be vigilant; because your adversary the devil
walks about like a roaring lion seeking whom he may
devour" (I Peter 4:12, 5:8). Moving into the Spirit-
filled life is to move into confrontation with the enemy.
But don't hesitate and never fear; for "You are of God,
little children, and have overcome them, because He
who is in you is greater than he who is in the world"
(I John 4:4).

Every point of spiritual advance is countered by
one of Satan's attempt to check that forward move-
ment. Doubt is a common weapon. For example, when
you first received Christ, didn't you find the Adversary
attempting to dissuade you as to the reality of your
salvation? When you have taken a step of faith, have
you ever been tormented by the question, "Can I be

50

sure God's Word is reliable?" And among the most common experiences I have found true to believers who have been recently filled with the Spirit is Satan's accusation: "Who do you think you are? You haven't *really* been filled!" Then he will often cite your weaknesses — a logical tactic since he is aware of your new resource of strength. If he can get you to wonder about the reality of what you have received he can force you on the defensive just at the time Christ has especially prepared you for attack.

An insight from the Word on this strategic device the Devil uses is notably present in his conversation with Jesus. When he says, "If You are the Son of God" (v. 3), the word "if" literally means *"since."* In short, even in approaching Jesus, the Adversary employs a defiance intended to intimidate. It's as though he is saying, "Since you're supposed to be someone so special . . ." or "Who do you think *YOU* are?" He still uses the same ruse, and too easily we back down and we whisper inwardly, "Perhaps I'm not as specifically prepared as I thought." But Jesus' bold responses would better recommend our equal boldness. When assailed by the Enemy's effort at challenging your authority in Christ, you may freely reply: "I AM special. I am a redeemed son/daughter of the Most High God. And furthermore, I resist all fear and doubt in the Name of my Lord — Jesus Christ of Nazareth! He's more special than anyone, anytime and anywhere, and I am complete in Him!"

TWO: Beware of any inclination to be self-serving.

In the light of the fact that Jesus was just concluding his forty-day fast, the Devil's suggestion that Jesus turn the stones to bread was a very practical temptation. There would have been nothing improper about Christ's partaking of bread; and on the face of it there was no reason to deny His right to work a miracle. But Jesus rejects the Devil's proposition, and in doing so provides us with at least this insight: the powerful resources of Spirit-filled living provide occasion for selfish use of your gifts unless you keep them under God's rulership.

Perhaps the earliest temptation the newly Spirit-filled face is the desire to flaunt their experience. There are so many ways this can be attempted, and with reasonable social grace. But at the heart, the honest-to-God believer knows when he is making the effort to "slip something in"; to seek to use his spiritual experience as a credential demonstrating some supposed status of added maturity or superiority above others. The primary and ultimate evidence of the Holy Spirit in anyone's life is *love,* and love will never seek its own advantage or do anything to inflate its own importance (I Cor. 13:4, 5).

THREE: If the power of the Holy Spirit is in your life, you don't have to prove it.

The craft of the serpent is to worm his way into position so that what he suggests appears spiritual: notice the Devil's quotation of Scripture to Jesus (v. 6). Of course, Jesus reads the Liar for what he is; for he will *never* seek to motivate you toward a good work or toward a point of obeying God's Word or will. When Satan dared Jesus to leap from the high place, his last interest was in demonstrating the power of God. So you can be certain that any presumptuous suggestion he makes to you is another case of the same lying effort to deceive.

A normal response to having received the fullness of the Holy Spirit is to gain an even deeper compassion for the lost, an even greater readiness to serve or an even heightened hunger for spiritual pursuit. Unfortunately, some who have not been taught the Adversary's devices have succumbed to presumption. Upon their introduction to Spirit-filled living they soon manifest an exaggerated or imbalanced effort at godliness. It is not uncommon to see them neglect good sense and practical duty, and to do so in the name of being "more spiritual." Worse yet, misled by the Devil into trying to prove their spiritual superiority, they do so to the pain of others who should be more sensitively and sensibly served. For example: One young man was so excited about his newly discovered dimension of power, insight and equipping through the Holy Spirit's overflow in his life, he suddenly left his job, uprooted his family and thrust himself out as an evangelist seeking public meetings. There's no question that the giftedness for such a ministry was present with him, but the *timing* and the *approach* to that ministry were miles off the mark. He ended up with a disillusioned wife, frustrated kids and considerable debt; and with it all, wondering why God had let him down. Of course, the failure wasn't God's. The failure was the successful ploy of the Adversary, prodding a devoted believer to "show your stuff, now that you're mighty in God."

You never need to "prove" the power of God in your life. The Lord may call you to steps of faith, but He never calls to flights of fancy. And if you ever need to test between which you may be feeling or hearing, there are mature and faith-filled spiritual leaders of sufficient depth and boldness of belief to hear your heart and counsel you.

FOUR: You will find new opportunities to declare the Lordship of Christ in your life.

When Jesus was pointedly challenged by Satan to bow to him, one wonders that such a suggestion was even made. Did Satan really think for one moment that God's Son would even consider the proposal — even with all the world's wealth and power offered as the lure? Whatever the answer may be, to Jesus' outright and complete refusal to so detestable a proposition we can see this lovely fact: that hellish summons only gave Jesus one more opportunity to indicate His full-hearted allegiance to the Father. His answer, "Get out of here! The Bible says to only worship and serve God!!" (v. 10), provides us with a healthy reminder: the flesh — though Spirit-filled and holy — still is dependent upon humility in worship and service before God to sustain its life in Him.

With respect to all that does take place when we are filled with the Spirit, one thing that does *not* occur is this: you are no less "flesh" for having been Spirit-filled. Paul's letter to the Galatians takes up that theme: "Having begun in the Spirit, do you think you can become complete and mature through the energy of the flesh?" (Galatians 3:3). To the Romans he cautioned, "If you live according to the flesh you will die; but if by the Spirit you put to death the deeds of the body, you will live" (Romans 8:13). Both of these words of counsel were directed to people who understood what being Spirit-filled meant. And by them, we are clearly warned that with all the joy, the power, the love and the thrill — none of these features of fullness pre-empts a continual monitoring of the flesh. The flesh will *always* seek its own way, and though the vessel is Spirit-filled, the vessel is still "flesh."

This is not to suggest that the presence of the Spirit makes no difference at all, for His infilling does indeed. The very point in view is that the fullness of the Spirit will bring increasingly additional opportunities for you to newly and freshly declare the Lordship of Jesus in your life. New confrontation with your self-ishness, pride or carnality — all will be faced. And when you do, remember that the power you have been given is only for serving Him — not yourself.

FIVE: Keeping full of God's Word is the best way to keep filled with God's Spirit.

The recurrence in this text of these words falling from Jesus' lips, "It is written . . . it is written . . . it is written," is an inescapable commentary on the pathway of Spirit-filled living. Jesus meets each situation with the Word of God. Taken in like manner into our hand, the Word becomes a flashing sword in the grip of a warrior, slicing through the froth of superficiality, cutting through the flesh of carnality and striking down the Adversary.

Such an immediate availability of the Word when battle strikes or when temptation flares is not the result of casual reading. Feeding upon the Word with regular habit, as certainly as one usually keeps regular mealtimes, is not only a powerful practice, but it is specifically taught in this text:

> Man shall not live by bread alone, but by every word which proceeds from the mouth of God (v. 4).

The essential point of understanding is that we are not dealing with a generalized or academic approach to the Bible. *Hearing* and *studying* the Word of God are both very desirable practices, and *both* are taught in the Scriptures. But hearing without *doing* and studying without *applying* are dangerously potential to even the most sincere among us (James 1:22). What keeps the Word of God *at hand* — ready for confrontation with flesh or devil — is allowing the Holy Spirit to infuse It into your spiritual system. Spirit-filled living calls for hearing, studying, doing and applying, and all become joyfully dynamic with the Holy Spirit's aid. There's nothing more fulfilling nor more certain to integrate the spirit of the Word into the substance of your living, than singing the Word to life through obedience to these words:

> Let the word of Christ dwell in you richly in all wisdom, teaching and admonishing one another in psalms and hymns and spiritual songs, singing with grace in your hearts to the Lord. Colossians 3:16

The pathway of promised life in the Spirit is one inviting us to learn to walk in God's wisdom and by God's power. Periodic warfare gains accumulated victories, while interim seasons of rejoicing are preparatory for our next conflict unto conquest. It's an unlimited journey into joy, with a ceaseless promise of hope:

> The path of the just is as a shining light, growing brighter and brighter unto the perfect day.
>   Proverbs 4:18

Chapter 7

The Panorama of the Promise

There is always the danger that, in describing our human experience of God's working in our lives, however unintentionally, we reduce our view of Him to a humanistic level — "God to our size," so to speak. Of course, God is not offended at our need to perceive of Him in human terms, for that is the very reason He became flesh. In the Person of Jesus, He came to us, becoming touchable by and understandable to all mankind.

Yet when we speak of the limited and finite frame of one human being receiving "the fullness of the Holy Spirit," we are attempting to express what words cannot actually describe with precision. The words we use *are* scriptural, but the concept is spiritual and it's good to understand its meaning.

To begin, being "filled" with God certainly does not mean that "all there is of God" has been fit into a human being. What it does mean is that:

the *essence* of His nature,

the *resource* of His power, and

the *presence* of His Person

have come to abide within us in a real and personal way.

Just as a child's bucket may be filled with water from the ocean as he stands on the shore, while the enormity of the sea is yet undiminished by his having filled his pail, so God's greatness exceeds whatever of Himself He pours into us.

When we receive of His fullness, the Holy Spirit comes in as but "an earnest of our inheritance; a down payment, or a guarantee of more to come, a small beginning of all that is in store" (Ephesians 1:14). Beyond that, the Bible says infinite abundance awaits us in the indescribable future, for "in the ages to come He might show the exceeding riches of His grace . . . in Christ Jesus" (Ephesians 2:7).

The prospect of an eternity to grow in our grasp of the goodness of God is a part of our inheritance in Christ. And yet, a very present feature of His grace is that He has opened to us *now* a constantly expanding resource of His life and fullness. This is especially true since you have opened to the full working of His Holy Spirit, and He has come in power to expand and expedite that life-flow.

The unfolding panorama of promise before each newly Spirit-filled believer opens your opportunity to move into (1) the *deepened experience* of the fruit of the Holy Spirit, and into (2) the *dynamic exercise* of His gifts. Although entire books are written on the subject of the Holy Spirit's fruit and gifts, at least an introductory overview of these provisions of God is presented here. This brief overview gives the foundational texts concerning each. They are set side by side for comparison, with the list of the nine provisions each category — the *Fruit* and the *Gifts* — affords.

The Fruit of the Spirit	The Gifts of the Spirit

Text:
Galatians 5:22, 23

Text:
I Corinthians 12:7-11

But the fruit of the Spirit is love, joy, peace, long-suffering, kindness, goodness, faithfulness, gentleness, self-control. Against such there is no law.

But the manifestation of the Spirit is given to each one for the profit of all: for to one is given the word of wisdom through the Spirit, to another the word of knowledge through the same Spirit, to another faith by the same Spirit, to another gifts of healings by the same Spirit, to another the working of miracles, to another prophecy, to another discerning of spirits, to another different kinds of tongues, to another the interpretation of tongues.

Text:
Ephesians 5:8-10

For you were once darkness, but now you are light in the Lord. Walk as children of light (for the fruit of the Spirit is in all goodness, righteousness and truth), proving what is acceptable to the Lord.

Fruit:
Love
Joy
Peace
Longsuffering
Kindness
Goodness
Faithfulness
Gentleness
Self-control

Gifts:
A word of wisdom
A word of knowledge
Faith
Healings
Working of miracles
Prophecy
Discerning of spirits
Tongues
Interpretation of tongues

Purpose:

The fruit of the Spirit focuses on the PERSON of Christ being manifest IN our life for HIM.

Purpose:

The gifts of the Spirit focus on the POWER of Christ being manifest THROUGH our life for Him.

Because of the fact that the fruit of the Spirit involves one's character, as compared with the gifts which involve divinely given abilities, there is a tendency of some people to prioritize or to neglect one at the expense of the other.

For example, some will say, "How you live for Christ is more important than what you do for Him. The fruit is more important." While another will say, "There is so great a need for powerful help in acting to meet human need, let's get on with gifts; fruit can grow later." But we should be careful to note that God's Word does not prioritize one above the other. Even the fact that they number the same — nine each — seems to be a pointer toward seeing God's heavenly balance on the issue.

We can be used in the gifts while we grow in the fruit of the Spirit. All of these processes are for us *now*. They are all of *grace* and they are all for Jesus Christ's glory. Open to both — fully and completely. Learn what you can and move ahead in Spirit-filled life, fruitfulness and ministry.

Perhaps the most important thing we might learn about all these attributes and abilities is this: *none of them are permanent in the sense that they become automatic.*

For example, the fruit of love can easily rot on the vine of a person's life if it is not nourished by today's fresh filling of the Spirit. Further, *no* gift of the Spirit is intended to become your private possession; for each is given to *minister* — that is, to give away, not to keep. So today's operation in the gifts of the Spirit doesn't qualify me for tomorrow — unless I keep freshly filled with the Spirit.

Keeping Full of the Holy Spirit

A comparative study of the life, ministry and prayer of the Early Church in the Book of Acts shows that those who were filled with the Spirit at Pentecost, had recurrent "fillings" with the Spirit on later occasions. (See Acts 2:4; 4:8; 4:31; and compare 9:17 with

13:9). This is not a commentary on the Holy Spirit's lack of commitment to us, as though He were moving in and out of those He indwells or infills. When He comes in fullness, He comes to *abide;* and He *remains* with us: "But the anointing which you have received from Him abides in you" (I John 2:27).

And yet there is a very real human capacity to lose our *sense* of His presence, or to somehow grieve the Spirit through insensitivity or disobedience. There is also a tremendous "drain off" that occurs through the daily business of our personal duties or through the pursuit of our spiritual service for Christ. The reservoir of heaven is abundantly adequate and always full, but on our side of things the channel of our own soul seems limited to receiving just *today's* supply. Paul spoke this, describing to the Philippians his own ability to survive the rigors of imprisonment, but *only* as he received "the supply of the Spirit of Christ" (Phil. 1:19).

So in this light, it is understandable that we are called to learn a daily walk of dependency, and a regular pattern of *re*-filling. The Ephesians were commanded, "Keep on being filled with the Holy Spirit" (Eph. 5:18); and the present imperative form of the verb makes the literal command read, *"Be continually being filled!"* With that command, another prospect on the panorama of promised-life in the Spirit unfolds: it's a summons to experience the ongoing beauty and endless glory which await those who will "keep coming back for more."

There is a pattern of life that will insure continual fullness of the Spirit, and it is maintained through three basics: (1) worship and praise, (2) feeding on the Word and (3) faithful obedience. Take these three rules of life and apply them, and there is no reason you ever need be less than "full of faith and of the Holy Spirit" (Acts 6:5).

1. *Worship and Praise*

The command of Ephesians 5 just quoted gives a simple directive to much *singing,* ". . . with psalms and hymns and spiritual songs, singing and making melody in your heart to the Lord" (v. 19). This parallels the Apostle's observation about his own life of praise and worship: "I will sing with the Spirit and I will sing with the understanding also" (I Cor. 14:15). It is not only *refreshing* to enter the Lord's presence with daily worship, it is also *refilling*. Song-filled, private, Holy Spirit-enabled praise is a key to keep renewed — freshly filled with the Spirit.

2. *Feeding on the Word*

In Peter's second letter, he writes of the Lord:

"His divine power has given to us all things that pertain to life and godliness, through the knowledge of Him who called us by glory and virtue, by which have been given to us exceedingly great and precious promises, that through these you may be partakers of the divine nature . . ."
II Peter 1:3, 4

The distilled truth of these words is this: the precious promises of God's holy Word are a resource for keeping full of the holy nature of God. His power "has given us" what we need. Now we need only to "be partakers" of that ongoing grace through receiving regular input of the Word.

3. *Faithful Obedience*

It is impossible to keep filled with the Holy Spirit and walk in willful disobedience at the same time. The biblical commands, (1) "Do not grieve the Holy Spirit" (Eph. 4:30), and (2) "Do not quench the Spirit" (I Thess. 5:19) point up this fact. When the Holy Spirit is grieved He will cause you to know it. He will not abandon you but He will signal you concerning whatever action, thought or attitude displeases Him.

Confession and obedience entertain His continued presence. But indifference or rebellion can quench Him; that is, drown out His voice or suffocate the flame of His power.

Keep sensitively obedient . . . and obediently sensitive. The reward is ongoing fullness with His abiding presence and power.

An increase of the power of the Holy Spirit is the guaranteed, ongoing potential to all who not only open their hearts to His fullness, but who will continue to learn the *life* of Spirit-filled possibilities. Just as you have come to Jesus to be filled, walk with Jesus and *keep* filled. The recurrent surgings of the Holy Spirit will sweep over you daily, and keep you ever-prepared for Christ's highest purpose

for all of your life . . .
  and in all of His will.

ALL MY DAYS

All my days I want to live here
  At the fountainhead of life
Always drinking in the fullness
  of the Spirit of Jesus Christ.

All my being in submission
  To His Word and to His will,
All my spirit opened heavenward
  That His love my vessel fill.

Spirit-filled I ask to be, Lord,
  Spirit-filled I want to stay.
Ever, always, constant, steady,
  Filled with power and filled with praise.

— J.W.H.

Questions People Ask About
Being Spirit-filled

Years of pastoral ministry have surfaced common questions related to being Spirit-filled. This brief series of questions and answers by Pastor Hayford is provided for your study and help.

"What is the sin against the Holy Spirit?"

There is a remarkable recurrence of inquiry on this question; concern by people over "the unpardonable sin," or "the sin against the Holy Spirit." It is certainly understandable since any sin that had no point of forgiveness with God would be the first one any thoughtful person would want to know of so as to be certain to avoid.

The grounds for the question are in the Word, because Jesus Himself spoke of a sin for which there is no forgiveness. The Scripture reads:

> *Therefore I say to you, every sin and blasphemy will be forgiven men, but the blasphemy against the Spirit will not be forgiven men. Anyone who speaks a word against the Son of Man, it will be forgiven him; but whoever speaks against the Holy Spirit, it will not be forgiven him, either in this age or in the age to come.*
>
> Matt. 12:31, 32; Mark 3:28-30; Luke 12:10

There are two definitions that are given of this sin. First, the most obvious is any word a person would speak that was forthrightly blasphemous against the Holy Spirit — the Third Person of the Trinity. Exactly how someone might do that is subject to interpretation, consequently a widely diverse description of that action exists among believers.

However, Jesus seems to make it clear in the context of the passages that the essence of this sin lies in attributing the work of the Holy Spirit to Satan (Mark 3:30). For example, of recent years there have been some who have attributed the exercise of some spiritual gifts to demons, and others have been quick to say those making such an ascription have committed this unpardonable sin. That seems doubtful, however, for it appears in the situation Jesus addressed that something deeper than theological misunderstanding was involved. In the text, the heart of the matter was human resistance against God's present work; resistance to the point that hardened hearts insisting on their own righteousness as opposed to God's working. The Pharisees virtually made themselves God by declaring Jesus' doings as of the Devil. In other words, they determined that the Holy Spirit at work through Jesus was so offensive to them that in making a judgment against Him, they were taking the same position as Lucifer: "I will be as God" (Isa. 14:12-15). For this — establishing one's own rightness in opposition to God's — there is no forgiveness. God Himself has hereby been removed or overruled by the individual's own order of things; therefore, eternal loss is the only option remaining. It is this conclusion that has led some to take an alternate position concerning the definition of this sin.

Some see the unpardonable sin as the individual's rejection of Jesus Christ as God's Messiah, the Savior of the world. Since the ministry of the Holy Spirit is to testify to the fact of Jesus' Saviorhood and mankind's need of Him (John 16:8-11), it is argued that the willful rejection of the Holy Spirit's efforts at bringing you to Christ is the sin against the Holy Spirit. Therefore, of course, no salvation — no forgiveness is available (John 14:6; Acts 4:12).

In any case, regardless of the precise definition, the sin against the Holy Spirit is *not* a matter that needs to be a preoccupying problem for any sincere believer. My experience of years has taught me that there are inevitably a certain number of earnest, seeking, semi-informed souls who will become trapped by the fear that they have committed this sin. Lying spirits and human guilt combine to reinforce whatever syndrome of rejection has been laid on their mind.

65

Wherever I am confronted by such a person, who — whether weeping or stolidly passive by reason of their being convinced they are guilty of this unforgiveable sin — I offer this answer.

If you are concerned as to whether you have committed the unpardonable sin, you haven't. The very fact that you care, and that you hope you haven't committed it, is evidence in itself that:

(1) the Holy Spirit is still dealing with your heart, and

(2) therefore He is ready to bring you into peace and forgiveness which are both fully available to you.

If the lie persists, by whatever voice — internal mocking or condemning fear — speak against it in the Name of Jesus Christ of Nazareth. Through the Blood of His Cross, declare your full acceptance of His saving, atoning death and resurrection life as your grounds for salvation and acceptance by the Heavenly Father. Don't let Satan have a field day by distorting a truth which has nothing whatsoever to do with you. He — the Devil — *has* committed this sin, and it is not surprising that he tries to spread his hopeless despair to others. Instead, if you or anyone you counsel is tormented by his ensnaring device, resist the Devil and require him to flee from you. Stand in the liberty wherewith the Lord Jesus Christ has made us free, and rejoice in the blessings of His mercy, His forgiveness and His abiding love! (I Peter 5:8, 9; Galatians 5:1; I Peter 1:6-9).

"How holy must one be to qualify for the fullness of the Spirit?"

Acts 2:38, 39 makes clear that being filled with the Holy Spirit is a *gift*. It also establishes that it is a *promised* gift to everyone — to anyone who comes to Christ in repentance and who follows Christ in water baptism.

This promise is offered on the same terms as salvation — our new birth and forgiveness of sins. Beyond that, there is no preliminary qualification of special merit or holiness required to receive the fullness of the Holy Spirit.

In this respect it may be helpful to take special notice of the difference between "the *gift* of the Holy Spirit" (Acts 2:38) and "the *gifts* of the Holy Spirit" (I Corinthians 12:7-11). The *gift* (singular) is the Holy Spirit Himself, given by the Father (Luke 11:13), to all who obey Him (Acts 5:32), and poured forth by the hand of Jesus His Son (John 1:33; Acts 2:33).

The primary qualifying factor that Christ reveals for receiving the fullness of God is a genuine hunger and thirst for His righteousness — the pure power of His working (Matthew 5:6).

"May a person be filled with the Holy Spirit without being baptized in water?"

The overwhelming work of the Spirit on the occasion Peter preached to the household of Cornelius (Acts 10:24-48) makes it clear that water baptism is not a legal requirement for receiving the fullness of the Holy Spirit. But at the same time, the immediacy with which Peter instructed those who had just been filled to be baptized in water at once, indicates the importance of *both* in the divine order of things.

The notion that "Holy Spirit baptism" (or any other spiritual experience) might remove the need for water baptism is a deception. It suggests a status system which puts higher value on one point of obedience than another. We are taught to do both: (1) be baptized in water (Acts 2:38) and (2) be baptized in the Holy Spirit (Acts 1:5; John 1:33).

"What is the difference between 'the Baptism with the Holy Spirit,' 'being filled with the Holy Spirit' and 'becoming Spirit-filled'?"

These are generally interchangeable terms, and

the fact that a variety of phrases is used for the same spiritual experience shouldn't bother us. A rigid, legal insistence of terms may become religiously perfect, but the experience which is indicated is more important than the set of words used to describe it. For example, when someone "receives Christ as Savior," that experience is also frequently described as "being saved," "being born again" or "being converted."

It is possible to use *both* (1) biblical phraseology and (2) descriptive phraseology. Perhaps one would usually prefer the biblical terms, but there is nothing in the Bible that disallows the use of our own words in describing our experience. The only rule should be that we always go back to the Bible as the *standard* of our experience, never letting either human terms or human experience become the standard by itself. To do so is to eventually fall into humanistic practices without scriptural basis, and eventually to fall into confusion and error.

"Doesn't the Bible say that every believer is 'baptized by one spirit into one body,' and thereby every believer should be said to have already been baptized with the Holy Spirit when they are saved; i.e., when they received Christ?"

This perfectly understandable question, based on I Corinthians 12:13, is often raised by people who object to being invited as believers in Christ to receive the Baptism with the Holy Spirit. While I do not use the same terminology, I generally accept their preference that the term "Holy Spirit Baptism" be reserved for that event to which they refer — namely, their new birth.

Nonetheless, there is ample evidence in the Word that this term is used for the occasion at which a person is *filled* with the Holy Spirit. John 1:33 relates this ministry as "Baptizer with the Holy Spirit" as a distinct work of Christ from His ministry as "Lamb of God who takes away the sin of the world" (John 1:29, 33). Further, Jesus Himself urged His disciples to remain in Jerusalem, for "you shall be baptized with the Holy Spirit not many days from now" (Acts 1:5). Many feel that these texts indicate a difference between: (1) the baptism BY the Holy Spirit and (2) the baptism IN the Spirit. The first is the Holy Spirit's baptism, as He brings the repentant believer unto and into Christ. The second is Jesus' baptism as He fills and overflows His own with the power of the Holy Spirit.

It is probably best not to labor with this to the point of division in the unity Jesus wants in the Body of His Church. The actual Greek preposition used in both texts is the same (en), and it is translatable either as "in," "with" or "by," depending upon the understood meaning of the text by the translator.

Irrespective of differences in terminology, however, the one inescapable fact is that the Word calls us to *both*, repentance and baptism in water (enter *into* Christ) *and* Holy Spirit fullness (given us *by* Christ). To fail to seek the fullness of the Holy Spirit on the grounds of one's supposition that their salvation already accomplishes that, is to either misunderstand Scripture or misconstrue it.

"What is the place of 'tongues' in the work of the Holy Spirit?"

The spectrum of opinion runs all the way from sturdy opposition to any biblical practice of "speaking with tongues" to an insistence that it is the first physical sign of a person's becoming Spirit-filled. This is unfortunate when we consider (1) the place that God gave this sign, (2) the statement Jesus made about it and (3) the observations Paul boldly declares.

First, that the Church was born at Pentecost with this sign upon its lips ("they were all filled with the Holy Spirit and began to speak with other tongues as the Spirit gave them utterance" — Acts 2:4) makes it impossible to relegate it to the insignificant. With His creative resources as God Almighty Creator, He might have designed any one of ten thousand things as indicators or signals of His working on so historic an occasion as the beginning of The Church. As it is, He chose "speaking with tongues" as one phenomenon to be included, and considering its recurrence elsewhere in the Early Church, it cannot be consigned to a "one-time-only" concept. God must see some importance in the practice, otherwise we must say He certainly made a mistake starting the Church with it.

Second, Jesus prophesied that those who believe in Him "shall speak with new tongues" (Mark 16:17). Were it not for the miracle nature of the sign as it occurs throughout the rest of the New Testament following this prophecy, we might have thought He was merely foretelling the fact that people of various nations would come to faith in Him. But the evidence of the Scriptures will not allow us to honestly accept the meaning of His forecast about "tongues" as only being native languages of believers in nations newly evangelized.

Third, quite remarkably, in spite of the fact that he had some difficulty with one congregation who ignorantly violated the proper use of "tongues," the Apostle Paul is still very bold to encourage the personal use of and expectancy toward this miracle of language in prayer and praise.

While on the one hand objecting to the Corinthians' indiscriminate public use of the capacity to speak with tongues (I Cor. 14:23), he freely expresses his regular use of spiritual language in private: "I thank my God I speak with tongues more than all of you" (14:18). Paul unhesitatingly expresses his willingness to sing *both* with his understanding *and* with his spirit (14:15). Further, he affirms the validity of the exercise of tongues *if* — if it doesn't overshadow the exercise of gifts that serve the understanding (14:5).

When Paul concludes the 14th Chapter of I Corinthians with a direct injunction to NOT prohibit the exercise of speaking with tongues (14:39) while requiring that public utterance *must* be disciplined and interpreted (14:27, 28), it seems that a vital, balanced teaching has been accomplished.

"Is there a sign that a person has been filled with the Spirit?"

The New Testament incidents where believers are specifically said to be filled with the Spirit help us answer this question. These narratives do contain clear evidence of at least one fact: the fullness of the Holy Spirit will manifest in something holy and something powerful. Study the cases:

(1) At Pentecost the miracle of worshipping God in new languages occurred (Acts 2:1-13).

(2) At Samaria the evidence of the text (Acts 8:9-24) clearly indicates that something sufficiently remarkable occurred to capture Simon's attention. His carnal quest to buy the power to confer the Holy Spirit upon people was not without the potential presence of some visible, physical manifestation. So carnal a proposition could not have been prompted by his appreciation for some invisible, internalized experience among those he saw.

(3) In Acts 10:44 following Peter's ministry to Cornelius' household, the Holy Spirit "fell upon them" and they spoke with tongues and prophesied. Both these manifestations are among the nine gifts of the Holy Spirit listed in I Corinthians 12. This clearly suggests that, at the very least, "gifts" of the Spirit might be expected to manifest when a believer receives the "gift" of the Spirit (Acts 2:39).

(4) Paul's ministering of the truth of the fullness of the Holy Spirit to the Ephesian

disciples also resulted in their speaking with tongues (Acts 19:1-6).

The significance of the four cases cited is that they are each *initiating* experiences; that is, those being filled with the Holy Spirit are experiencing their first taste of that fullness. This is not to be confused with the "refillings" which occur in such passages as Acts 4:8; 4:31; 13:9 and 13:52. Neither can we make a comparison with occasions of people being filled with the Spirit prior to Pentecost; such as Old Testament cases, or even New Testament occasions like Zacharias (Luke 1:67), Elizabeth (Luke 1:41), Mary (Luke 1:35) or John the Baptist (Luke 1:15).

This is only a difficult question to answer in the light of the arguments and misunderstandings which have plagued the Church on this subject. Sincere hearts do not want to violate the Holy Spirit of unity in the Body, and yet honest minds cannot deny the evidence in the Word of God: something supernatural ought to be expected when a person is initially filled with the Spirit.

To forge formula and impose it on the Body is ultimately to reduce a precious, spontaneous experience to religious rigidity. And yet to remove the miracle dimension of expectancy from this experience is to reduce it to formalized tradition.

To my view it is best that we open to *Jesus* Himself — He is the Baptizer with the Holy Spirit (John 1:33). When love *for* Him becomes our motive and love *from* Him is poured upon us, there will be room for the Holy Spirit to work in fullness *and* in power. Let us hesitate to impose our doctrinal traditions or our dogmatic demands on those who honestly seek the Spirit's fullness. And neither let us back away from any work of the Spirit which may humble our pride, cast out our fears or melt our hearts.

"What is 'praying in the Spirit' or 'praying with the Spirit'?"

Examples of this terminology are found in I Corinthians 14:15 and Ephesians 6:18:

> What is the result then? I will pray with the spirit and I will also pray with the understanding. I will sing with the spirit and I will also sing with the understanding.

> Praying always with all prayer and supplication in the Spirit, being watchful to this end with all perseverance and supplication for all saints.

First, we should establish that all prayer uttered from the heart is heard by the Living God, no matter how weak or desperate the call (Psalm 86:7). Further, all prayer spoken in Jesus' Name is effective (John 14:13, 14; Acts 2:21). There are not some kinds of prayer that are more worthy than others. God's heart is open to those who call upon Him, and He does not differentiate between "the spiritual prayers" and "the other ones."

But the multiplied dimensions of prayer are diverse, with a wide spectrum ranging from the basic request for daily bread to the bold attack of prayer in spiritual warfare. Devotional intimacy, praise-filled worship, contrite confession, joyous song, practical petition, insight-filled intercession and spiritual conflict against demonic strongholds — all these are prayer forms, and the growing believer will grow in them. (See note at end of this section.)

There are times that the *intensity* of prayer (see Ephesians 6:10-18, "wrestling") is such that a broadened dimension of prayer is needed. This may be manifest in *fervency* (James 5:16), i.e. "heated, impassioned prayer" offered in one's native tongue, or as Paul said, he would pray on some occasions "with the Spirit." The fact that he is contrasting prayer *"with the Spirit"* with prayer *"with the understanding,"* makes it clear in the context of the passage (I Corinthians 15) that he is referring to the use of "tongues" at certain

73

times in one's private prayer life.

It would be incomplete to describe "praying with, or in the Spirit" as *always* being "with tongues." But, it would also be incomplete to describe it as *never* involving that exercise.

"How may the gifts of the Holy Spirit be received and exercised?"

Because the understanding of the Holy Spirit's gifts and their function is so broad a subject, this abbreviated answer is only intended to prompt the faith that *you are* a candidate for their exercise. I can only encourage you to pursue such with an expectant heart.

The Bible says to "covet" spiritual gifts (i.e., "strongly desire" — I Corinthians 14:1). That alone is evidence of God's desire that we move into the employment of these resources.

The key to all Holy Spirit operations is hunger and thirst, as Jesus said: "Blessed are those who hunger and thirst after righteousness for they shall be filled" (Matthew 5:6). This is not only a condition to *being* "filled," it is the ongoing condition for *living* in His fullness.

The gifts of the Holy Spirit are fully available, and He is more than ready to distribute them *to* us and *through* us. "But one and the same Spirit works all these things, distributing to each one individually as He wills" (I Corinthians 12:11; see verses 1-11).

"As He wills" does not imply He is stingy; grudgingly withholding gifts for the few who qualify. To the contrary, gifts of the Holy Spirit (Greek: *"charis*mata") are functions of God's grace (Greek: *"charis"*). The very inclusion of the word "grace" in this word for "gift" indicates the free availability of the Holy Spirit's operation and power to those who keep open to Him.

There is no status among the gifts. Because they are of necessity listed in a sequence, some argue that some gifts of the Spirit are more worthy than others. But the fruit of the Spirit is also listed in an order, yet no one is foolish enough to suggest one characteristic to be more or less prized or significant than another. Also, you may occasionally hear someone suggest one gift as more to be sought than another (example: wisdom); or to refer to "tongues" as "the least of the gifts." Of course, that isn't scriptural; in fact, that quotation ("least of the gifts") is not in the Bible, but is of human invention.

The Holy Spirit makes the whole spectrum of gifts available to the wholeheartedly open. So, the way you may receive the gifts of the Holy Spirit is to live in that openness and to exercise them in the spirit of His love.

An exposition and explanation of the many aspects of prayer may be studied in the author's book, "Prayer Is Invading The Impossible," released by both *Bridge* and *Ballantine* publishing companies. To obtain a copy, write to: Ballantine Books, 201 East Fiftieth Street, New York, NY 10022.

THE ACTS
of the Apostles

Because the Book of Acts records the action and activities, the spirit and thrust of the Spirit-filled Church which Jesus birthed, this Book is included for your study. Be refreshed and be expectant of such workings of God in your own life, your own family, your own congregation and *in our* time — Today!

— J.W.H.

ACTS 1

The former account I made, O Theophilus, of all that Jesus began both to do and teach,

2 until the day in which He was taken up, after He through the Holy Spirit had given commandments to the apostles whom He had chosen,

3 to whom He also presented Himself alive after His suffering by many infallible proofs, being seen by them during forty days and speaking of the things pertaining to the kingdom of God.

4 And being assembled together with *them*, He commanded them not to depart from Jerusalem, but to wait for the Promise of the Father, "which," *He said,* "you have heard from Me;

5 "for John truly baptized with water, but you shall be baptized with the Holy Spirit not many days from now."

6 Therefore, when they had come together, they asked Him, saying, "Lord, will You at this time restore the kingdom to Israel?"

7 And He said to them, "It is not for you to know times or seasons which the Father has put in His own authority.

8 "But you shall receive power when the Holy Spirit has come upon you; and you shall be witnesses to Me in Jerusalem, and in all Judea and Samaria, and to the end of the earth."

9 Now when He had spoken these things, while they watched, He was taken up, and a cloud received Him out of their sight.

10 And while they looked steadfastly toward heaven as He went up, behold, two men stood by them in white apparel,

11 who also said, "Men of Galilee, why do you stand gazing up into heaven? This *same* Jesus, who was taken up from you into heaven, will so come in like manner as you saw Him go into heaven."

12 Then they returned to Jerusalem from the mount called Olivet, which is near Jerusalem, a Sabbath day's journey.

13 And when they had entered, they went up into the upper room where they were staying: Peter, James, John, and Andrew; Philip and Thomas; Bartholomew and Matthew; James *the son* of Alphaeus and Simon the Zealot; and Judas *the son* of James.

14 These all continued with one accord in prayer and supplication, with the women and Mary the mother of Jesus, and with His brothers.

15 And in those days Peter stood up in the midst of the disciples (altogether the number of names was about a hundred and twenty), and said,

16 "Men *and* brethren, this Scripture had to be fulfilled, which the Holy Spirit spoke before by the mouth of David concerning Judas, who became a guide to those who arrested Jesus;

17 "for he was numbered with us and obtained a part in this ministry."

18 (Now this man purchased a field with the wages of iniquity; and falling headlong, he burst open in the middle and all his entrails gushed out.

19 And it became known to all those dwelling in Jerusalem; so that field is called in their own language, Akel Dama, that is, Field of Blood.)

20 "For it is written in the book of Psalms: 'Let his habitation be desolate, and let no one live in it'; and, 'Let another take his office.'

21 "Therefore, of these men who have accompanied us all the time that the Lord Jesus went in and out among us,

22 "beginning from the baptism of John to that day when He was taken up from us, one of these must become a witness with us of His resurrection."

23 And they proposed two: Joseph called Barsabas, who was surnamed Justus, and Matthias.

24 And they prayed and said, "You, O Lord, who know the hearts of all, show which of these two You have chosen

25 "to take part in this ministry and apostleship from which Judas by transgression fell, that he might go to his own place."

26 And they cast their lots, and the lot fell on Matthias. And he was numbered with the eleven apostles.

ACTS 2

Now when the Day of Pentecost had fully come, they were all with one accord in one place.

2 And suddenly there came a sound from heaven, as of a rushing mighty wind, and it filled the whole house where they were sitting.

3 Then there appeared to them divided tongues, as of fire, and *one* sat upon each of them.

4 And they were all filled with the Holy Spirit and began to speak with other tongues, as the Spirit gave them utterance.

5 Now there were dwelling in Jerusalem Jews, devout men, from every nation under heaven.

6 And when this sound occurred, the multitude came together, and were confused, because everyone heard them speak in his own language.

7 Then they were all amazed and marveled, saying to one another, "Look, are not all these who speak Galileans?

8 "And how *is it that* we hear, each in our own language in which we were born?

9 "Parthians and Medes and Elamites, those dwelling in Mesopotamia, Judea and Cappadocia, Pontus and Asia,

10 "Phrygia and Pamphylia, Egypt and the parts of Libya adjoining Cyrene, visitors from Rome, both Jews and proselytes,

11 "Cretans and Arabs — we hear them speaking in our own tongues the wonderful works of God."

12 So they were all amazed and perplexed, saying to one another, "Whatever could this mean?"

13 Others mocking said, "They are full of new wine."

14 But Peter, standing up with the eleven, raised his voice and said to them, "Men of Judea and all who dwell in Jerusalem, let this be known to you, and heed my words.

15 "For these are not drunk, as you suppose, since it is *only* the third hour of the day.

16 "But this is what was spoken by the prophet Joel:

17 'And it shall come to pass in the last days, says God, that I will pour out of My Spirit on all flesh; your sons and your daughters shall prophesy, your young men shall see visions, your old men shall dream dreams.

18 'And on My menservants and on My maidservants I will pour out My Spirit in those days; and they shall prophesy.

19 'I will show wonders in heaven above and signs in the earth beneath: blood and fire and vapor of smoke.

20 'The sun shall be turned into darkness, and the moon into blood, before the coming of the great and notable day of the Lord.

21 'And it shall come to pass *that* whoever calls on the name of the Lord shall be saved.'

22 "Men of Israel, hear these words: Jesus of Nazareth, a Man attested by God to you by miracles, wonders, and signs which God did through Him in your midst, as you yourselves also know —

23 "Him, being delivered by the determined counsel and foreknowledge of God, you have taken by lawless hands, have crucified, and put to death;

24 "whom God raised up, having loosed the pains of death, because it was not possible that He should be held by it.

25 "For David says concerning Him: '*I foresaw the Lord always before my face, for He is at my right hand, that I may not be shaken;*

26 '*therefore my heart rejoiced, and my tongue was glad; moreover my flesh will also rest in hope,*

27 '*because You will not leave my soul in Hades, nor will You allow Your Holy One to see corruption.*

28 '*You have made known to me the ways of life; You will make me full of joy in Your presence.*'

29 "Men *and* brethren, let *me* speak freely to you of the patriarch David, that he is both dead and buried, and his tomb is with us to this day.

30 "Therefore, being a prophet, and knowing that God had sworn with an oath to him that of the fruit of his body, according to the flesh, He would raise up the Christ to sit on his throne,

31 "he, foreseeing this, spoke concerning the resurrection of the Christ, that His soul was not left in Hades, nor did His flesh see corruption.

32 "This Jesus God has raised up, of which we are all witnesses.

33 "Therefore being exalted to the right hand of God, and having received from the Father the promise of the Holy Spirit, He poured out this which you now see and hear.

34 "For David did not ascend into the heavens, but he says himself: '*The Lord said to my Lord, "Sit at My right hand,*

35 "*till I make Your enemies Your footstool.*"

36 "Therefore let all the house of Israel know assuredly that God has made this Jesus, whom you crucified, both Lord and Christ."

37 Now when they heard *this*, they were cut to the heart, and said to Peter and the rest of the apostles, "Men *and* brethren, what shall we do?"

38 Then Peter said to them, "Repent, and let every one of you be baptized in the name of Jesus Christ for the remission of sins; and you shall receive the gift of the Holy Spirit.

39 "For the promise is to you and to your children, and to all who are afar off, as many as the Lord our God will call."

40 And with many other words he testified and exhorted them, saying, "Be saved from this perverse generation."

41 Then those who gladly received his word were baptized; and that day about three thousand souls were added *to them*.

42 And they continued steadfastly in the apostles' doctrine and fellowship, in the breaking of bread, and in prayers.

43 Then fear came upon every soul, and many wonders and signs were done through the apostles.

44 Now all who believed were together, and had all things in common,

45 and sold their possessions and goods, and divided them among all, as anyone had need.

46 So continuing daily with one accord in the temple, and breaking bread from house to house, they ate their food with gladness and simplicity of heart,

47 praising God and having favor with all the people. And the Lord added to the church daily those who were being saved.

ACTS 3

Now Peter and John went up together to the temple at the hour of prayer, the ninth *hour*.

2 And a certain man lame from his mother's womb was carried, whom they laid daily at the gate of the temple which is called Beautiful, to ask alms from those who entered the temple;

3 who, seeing Peter and John about to go into the temple, asked for alms.

4 And fixing his eyes on him, with John, Peter said, "Look at us."

5 So he gave them his attention, expecting to receive something from them.

6 Then Peter said, "Silver and gold I do not have, but what I do have I give you: In the name of Jesus Christ of Nazareth, rise up and walk."

7 And he took him by the right hand and lifted *him* up, and immediately his feet and ankle bones received strength.

8 So he, leaping up, stood and walked and entered the temple with them — walking, leaping, and praising God.

9 And all the people saw him walking and praising God.

10 Then they knew that it was he who sat begging alms at the Beautiful Gate of the temple; and they were filled with wonder and amazement at what had happened to him.

11 Now as the lame man who was healed held on to Peter and John, all the people ran together to them in the porch which is called Solomon's, greatly amazed.

12 So when Peter saw *it,* he responded to the people: "Men of Israel, why do you marvel at this? Or why look so intently at us, as though by our own power or godliness we had made this man walk?

13 "The God of Abraham, Isaac, and Jacob, the God of our fathers, glorified His Servant Jesus, whom you delivered up and denied in the presence of Pilate, when he was determined to let *Him* go.

14 "But you denied the Holy One and the Just, and asked for a murderer to be granted to you,

15 "and killed the Prince of life, whom God raised from the dead, of which we are witnesses.

16 "And His name, through faith in His name, has made this man strong, whom you see and know. Yes, the faith which *comes* through Him has given him this perfect soundness in the presence of you all.

17 "Yet now, brethren, I know that you did *it* in ignorance, as *did* also your rulers.

18 "But those things which God foretold by the mouth of all His prophets, that the Christ would suffer, He has thus fulfilled.

19 "Repent therefore and be converted, that your sins may be blotted out, so that times of refreshing may come from the presence of the Lord,

20 "and that He may send Jesus Christ, who was preached to you before,

21 "whom heaven must receive until the times of restoration of all things, which God has spoken by the mouth of all His holy prophets since the world began.

22 "For Moses truly said to the fathers, 'The Lord your God will raise up for you a Prophet like me from your brethren. Him you shall hear in all things, whatever He says to you.

23 'And it shall come to pass that every soul who will not hear that Prophet shall be utterly destroyed from among the people.'

24 "Yes, and all the prophets, from Samuel and those who follow, as many as have spoken, have also foretold these days.

25 "You are sons of the prophets, and of the covenant which God made with our fathers, saying to Abraham, 'And in your seed all the families of the earth shall be blessed.'

26 "To you first, God, having raised up His Servant Jesus, sent Him to bless you, in turning away every one *of you* from your iniquities."

ACTS 4

N ow as they spoke to the people, the priests, the captain of the temple, and the Sadducees came upon them,

2 being greatly disturbed that they taught the people and preached in Jesus the resurrection from the dead.

3 And they laid hands on them, and put *them* in custody until the next day, for it was already evening.

4 However, many of those who heard the word believed; and the number of the men came to be about five thousand.

5 And it came to pass, on the next day, that their rulers, elders, and scribes,

6 as well as Annas the high priest, Caiaphas, John, and Alexander, and as many as were of the family of the high priest, were gathered together at Jerusalem.

7 And when they had set them in the midst, they asked, "By what power or by what name have you done this?"

8 Then Peter, filled with the Holy Spirit, said to them, "Rulers of the people and elders of Israel:

9 "If we this day are judged for a good deed *done* to *the* helpless man, by what means he has been made well,

10 "let it be known to you all, and to all the people of Israel, that by the name of Jesus Christ of Nazareth, whom you crucified, whom God raised from the dead, by Him this man stands here before you whole.

11 "This is the *'stone which was rejected by you builders, which has become the chief cornerstone.'*

12 "Nor is there salvation in any other, for there is no other name under heaven given among men by which we must be saved."

13 Now when they saw the boldness of Peter and John, and perceived that they were uneducated and untrained men, they marveled. And they realized that they had been with Jesus.

14 And seeing the man who had been healed standing with them, they could say nothing against it.

15 But when they had commanded them to go aside out of the council, they conferred among themselves,

16 saying, "What shall we do to these men? For, indeed, that a notable miracle has been done through them *is* evident to all who dwell in Jerusalem, and we cannot deny *it*.

17 "But so that it spreads no further among the people, let us severely threaten them, that from now on they speak to no man in this name."

18 And they called them and commanded them

not to speak at all nor teach in the name of Jesus.

19 But Peter and John answered and said to them, "Whether it is right in the sight of God to listen to you more than to God, you judge.

20 "For we cannot but speak the things which we have seen and heard."

21 So when they had further threatened them, they let them go, finding no way of punishing them, because of the people, since they all glorified God for what had been done.

22 For the man was over forty years old on whom this miracle of healing had been performed.

23 And being let go, they went to their own *companions* and reported all that the chief priests and elders had said to them.

24 So when they heard that, they raised their voice to God with one accord and said: "Lord, You *are* God, who made heaven and earth and the sea, and all that is in them,

25 "who by the mouth of Your servant David have said: *'Why did the nations rage, and the people plot vain things?*

26 *'The kings of the earth took their stand, and the rulers were gathered together against the Lord and against His Christ.'*

27 "For truly against Your holy Servant Jesus, whom You anointed, both Herod and Pontius Pilate, with the Gentiles and the people of Israel, were gathered together

28 "to do whatever Your hand and Your purpose determined before to be done.

29 "Now, Lord, look on their threats, and grant to Your servants that with all boldness they may speak Your word,

30 "by stretching out Your hand to heal, and that signs and wonders may be done through the name of Your holy Servant Jesus."

31 And when they had prayed, the place where they were assembled together was shaken; and they

were all filled with the Holy Spirit, and they spoke the word of God with boldness.

32 Now the multitude of those who believed were of one heart and one soul; neither did anyone say that any of the things he possessed was his own, but they had all things in common.

33 And with great power the apostles gave witness to the resurrection of the Lord Jesus. And great grace was upon them all.

34 Nor was there anyone among them who lacked; for all who were possessors of lands or houses sold them, and brought the proceeds of the things that were sold,

35 and laid *them* at the apostles' feet; and they distributed to each as anyone had need.

36 And Joses, who was also named Barnabas by the apostles (which is translated Son of Encouragement), a Levite of the country of Cyprus,

37 having land, sold *it,* and brought the money and laid *it* at the apostles' feet.

ACTS 5

But a certain man named Ananias, with Sapphira his wife, sold a possession.

2 And he kept back *part* of the proceeds, his wife also being aware *of it,* and brought a certain part and laid *it* at the apostles' feet.

3 But Peter said, "Ananias, why has Satan filled your heart to lie to the Holy Spirit and keep back *part* of the price of the land for yourself?

4 "While it remained, was it not your own? And after it was sold, was it not in your own control? Why have you conceived this thing in your heart? You have not lied to men but to God."

5 Then Ananias, hearing these words, fell down and breathed his last. So great fear came upon all those who heard these things.

6 And the young men arose and wrapped him up, carried *him* out, and buried *him*.

7 Now it was about three hours later when his wife came in, not knowing what had happened.

8 And Peter answered her, "Tell me whether you sold the land for so much?" And she said, "Yes, for so much."

9 Then Peter said to her, "How is it that you have agreed together to test the Spirit of the Lord? Look, the feet of those who have buried your husband *are* at the door, and they will carry you out."

10 Then immediately she fell down at his feet and breathed her last. And the young men came in and found her dead, and carrying *her* out, buried *her* by her husband.

11 So great fear came upon all the church and upon all who heard these things.

12 And through the hands of the apostles many signs and wonders were done among the people. And they were all with one accord in Solomon's Porch.

13 Yet none of the rest dared join them, but the people esteemed them highly.

14 And believers were increasingly added to the Lord, multitudes of both men and women,

15 so that they brought the sick out into the streets and laid *them* on beds and couches, that at least the shadow of Peter passing by might fall on some of them.

16 Also a multitude gathered from the surrounding cities to Jerusalem, bringing sick people and those who were tormented by unclean spirits, and they were all healed.

17 Then the high priest rose up, and all those who *were* with him (which is the sect of the Sadducees), and they were filled with indignation,

18 and laid their hands on the apostles and put them in the common prison.

19 But at night an angel of the Lord opened the prison doors and brought them out, and said,

20 "Go, stand in the temple and speak to the people all the words of this life."

21 And when they heard *that,* they entered the temple early in the morning and taught. But the high priest and those with him came and called the council together, with all the elders of the children of Israel, and sent to the prison to have them brought.

22 But when the officers came and did not find them in the prison, they returned and reported,

23 saying, "Indeed we found the prison shut securely, and the guards standing outside before the doors; but when we opened them, we found no one inside!"

24 Now when the high priest, the captain of the temple, and the chief priests heard these things, they wondered what the outcome would be.

25 Then one came and told them, saying, "Look, the men whom you put in prison are standing in the temple and teaching the people!"

26 Then the captain went with the officers and brought them without violence, for they feared the people, lest they should be stoned.

27 And when they had brought them, they set *them* before the council. And the high priest asked them,

28 saying, "Did we not strictly command you not to teach in this name? And look, you have filled Jerusalem with your doctrine, and intend to bring this Man's blood on us!"

29 Then Peter and the *other* apostles answered and said: "We ought to obey God rather than men.

30 "The God of our fathers raised up Jesus whom you murdered by hanging on a tree.

31 "Him God has exalted to His right hand *to be* Prince and Savior, to give repentance to Israel and forgiveness of sins.

32 "And we are His witnesses to these things, and *so* also *is* the Holy Spirit whom God has given to those who obey Him."

33 When they heard *this,* they were furious and took counsel to kill them.

34 Then one in the council stood up, a Pharisee

named Gamaliel, a teacher of the law held in respect by all the people, and commanded them to put the apostles outside for a little while.

35 And he said to them: "Men of Israel, take heed to yourselves what you intend to do regarding these men.

36 "For some time ago Theudas rose up, claiming to be somebody. A number of men, about four hundred, joined him. He was slain, and all who obeyed him were scattered and came to nothing.

37 "After this man, Judas of Galilee rose up in the days of the census, and drew away many people after him. He also perished, and all who obeyed him were dispersed.

38 "And now I say to you, keep away from these men and let them alone; for if this plan or this work is of men, it will come to nothing;

39 "but if it is of God, you cannot overthrow it — lest you even be found to fight against God."

40 And they agreed with him, and when they had called for the apostles and beaten *them,* they commanded that they should not speak in the name of Jesus, and let them go.

41 So they departed from the presence of the council, rejoicing that they were counted worthy to suffer shame for His name.

42 And daily in the temple, and in every house, they did not cease teaching and preaching Jesus *as* the Christ.

ACTS 6

Now in those days, when *the number of* the disciples was multiplying, there arose a murmuring against the Hebrews by the Hellenists, because their widows were neglected in the daily distribution.

2 Then the twelve summoned the multitude of the disciples and said, "It is not desirable that we should leave the word of God and serve tables.

3 "Therefore, brethren, seek out from among you seven men of *good* reputation, full of the Holy Spirit and wisdom, whom we may appoint over this business;

4 "but we will give ourselves continually to prayer and to the ministry of the word."

5 And the saying pleased the whole multitude. And they chose Stephen, a man full of faith and the Holy Spirit, and Philip, Prochorus, Nicanor, Timon, Parmenas, and Nicolas, a proselyte from Antioch,

6 whom they set before the apostles; and when they had prayed, they laid hands on them.

7 And the word of God spread, and the number of the disciples multiplied greatly in Jerusalem, and a great many of the priests were obedient to the faith.

8 And Stephen, full of faith and power, did great wonders and signs among the people.

9 Then there arose some from what is called the Synagogue of the Freedmen (Cyrenians, Alexandrians, and those from Cilicia and Asia), disputing with Stephen.

10 And they were not able to resist the wisdom and the Spirit by which he spoke.

11 Then they secretly induced men to say, "We have heard him speak blasphemous words against Moses and God."

12 And they stirred up the people, the elders, and the scribes; and they came upon *him,* seized him, and brought *him* to the council.

13 They also set up false witnesses who said, "This man does not cease to speak blasphemous words against this holy place and the law;

14 "for we have heard him say that this Jesus of Nazareth will destroy this place and change the customs which Moses delivered to us."

15 And all who sat in the council, looking steadfastly at him, saw his face as the face of an angel.

ACTS 7

Then the high priest said, "Are these things so?"

2 And he said, "Men and brethren and fathers, listen: The God of glory appeared to our father Abraham when he was in Mesopotamia, before he dwelt in Haran,

3 "and said to him, *'Get out of your country and from your relatives, and come to a land that I will show you.'*

4 "Then he came out of the land of the Chaldeans and dwelt in Haran. And from there, when his father was dead, He moved him to this land in which you now dwell.

5 "And God gave him no inheritance in it, not even *enough* to set his foot on. But even when *Abraham* had no child, He promised to give it to him for a possession, and to his descendants after him.

6 "But God spoke in this way: that his descendants would sojourn in a foreign land, and that they would bring them into bondage and oppress *them* four hundred years.

7 *'And the nation to whom they will be in bondage I will judge,'* said God, *'and after that they shall come out and serve Me in this place.'*

8 "Then He gave him the covenant of circumcision; and so *Abraham* begot Isaac and circumcised him on the eighth day; and Isaac *begot* Jacob, and Jacob *begot* the twelve patriarchs.

9 "And the patriarchs, becoming envious, sold Joseph into Egypt. But God was with him

10 "and delivered him out of all his troubles, and gave him favor and wisdom in the presence of Pharaoh, king of Egypt; and he made him governor over Egypt and all his house.

11 "Now a famine and great trouble came over all the land of Egypt and Canaan, and our fathers found no sustenance.

12 "But when Jacob heard that there was grain in Egypt, he sent out our fathers first.

13 "And the second *time* Joseph was made known to his brothers, and Joseph's family became known to the Pharaoh.

14 "Then Joseph sent and called his father Jacob and all his relatives to *him,* seventy-five people.

15 "So Jacob went down to Egypt; and he died, he and our fathers.

16 "And they were carried back to Shechem and laid in the tomb that Abraham bought for a sum of money from the sons of Hamor, *the father* of Shechem.

17 "But when the time of the promise drew near which God had sworn to Abraham, the people grew and multiplied in Egypt

18 "till another king arose who did not know Joseph.

19 "This man dealt treacherously with our people, and oppressed our forefathers, making them expose their babies, so that they might not live.

20 "At this time Moses was born, and was well pleasing to God; and he was brought up in his father's house for three months.

21 "But when he was set out, Pharaoh's daughter took him away and brought him up as her own son.

22 "And Moses was learned in all the wisdom of the Egyptians, and was mighty in words and deeds.

23 "But when he was forty years old, it came into his heart to visit his brethren, the children of Israel.

24 "And seeing one of *them* suffer wrong, he defended and avenged him who was oppressed, and struck down the Egyptian.

25 "For he supposed that his brethren would have understood that God would deliver them by his hand, but they did not understand.

26 "And the next day he appeared to two of them as they were fighting, and *tried to* reconcile them, saying, 'Men, you are brethren; why do you wrong one another?'

27 "But he who did his neighbor wrong pushed him away, saying, 'Who made you a ruler and a judge over us?

28 'Do you want to kill me as you did the Egyptian yesterday?'

29 "Then, at this saying, Moses fled and became a sojourner in the land of Midian, where he had two sons.

30 "And when forty years had passed, an Angel of the Lord appeared to him in a flame of fire in a bush, in the wilderness of Mount Sinai.

31 "When Moses saw *it,* he marveled at the sight; and as he drew near to observe, the voice of the Lord came to him,

32 *"saying, 'I am the God of your fathers the God of Abraham, the God of Isaac, and the God of Jacob.'* And Moses trembled and dared not look.

33 *'Then the Lord said to him, "Take your sandals off your feet, for the place where you stand is holy ground.*

34 *"I have certainly seen the oppression of my people who are in Egypt; I have heard their groaning and have come down to deliver them. And now come, I will send you to Egypt." '*

35 "This Moses whom they rejected, saying, 'Who made you a ruler and a judge?' is the one God sent *to be* a ruler and a deliverer by the hand of the Angel who appeared to him in the bush.

36 "He brought them out, after he had shown wonders and signs in the land of Egypt, and in the Red Sea, and in the wilderness forty years.

37 "This is that Moses who said to the children of Israel, *'The Lord your God will raise up for you a Prophet like me from your brethren. Him you shall hear.'*

38 "This is he who was in the congregation in the wilderness with the Angel who spoke to him on Mount Sinai, and *with* our fathers, the one who received the living oracles to give to us,

39 "whom our fathers would not obey, but rejected. And in their hearts they turned back to Egypt,

40 "saying to Aaron, *'Make us gods to go before us;*

as for this Moses who brought us out of the land of Egypt, we do not know what has become of him.'

41 "And they made a calf in those days, offered sacrifices to the idol, and rejoiced in the works of their own hands.

42 "Then God turned and gave them up to worship the host of heaven, as it is written in the book of the Prophets: 'Did you offer Me slaughtered animals and sacrifices during forty years in the wilderness, O house of Israel?

43 'Yes, you took up the tabernacle of Moloch, and the star of your god Remphan, images which you made to worship; and I will carry you away beyond Babylon.'

44 "Our fathers had the tabernacle of witness in the wilderness, as He appointed, instructing Moses to make it according to the pattern that he had seen,

45 "which our fathers, having received it in turn, also brought with Joshua into the land possessed by the Gentiles, whom God drove out before the face of our fathers until the days of David,

46 "who found favor before God and asked to find a dwelling for the God of Jacob.

47 "But Solomon built Him a house.

48 "However, the Most High does not dwell in temples made with hands, as the prophet says:

49 'Heaven is My throne, and earth is My footstool. What house will you build for Me? says the Lord, or what is the place of My rest?

50 'Has My hand not made all these things?'

51 "You stiff-necked and uncircumcised in heart and ears! You always resist the Holy Spirit; as your fathers did, so do you.

52 "Which of the prophets did your fathers not persecute? And they killed those who foretold the coming of the Just One, of whom you now have become the betrayers and murderers,

53 "who have received the law by the direction of angels and have not kept it."

54 When they heard these things they were cut to the heart, and they gnashed at him with *their* teeth.

55 But he, being full of the Holy Spirit, gazed into heaven and saw the glory of God, and Jesus standing at the right hand of God,

56 and said, "Look! I see the heavens opened and the Son of Man standing at the right hand of God!"

57 Then they cried out with a loud voice, stopped their ears, and ran at him with one accord;

58 and they cast *him* out of the city and stoned *him.* And the witnesses laid down their clothes at the feet of a young man named Saul.

59 And they stoned Stephen as he was calling on *God* and saying, "Lord Jesus, receive my spirit."

60 Then he knelt down and cried out with a loud voice, "Lord, do not charge them with this sin." And when he had said this, he fell asleep.

ACTS 8

N ow Saul was consenting to his death. At that time a great persecution arose against the church which was at Jerusalem; and they were all scattered throughout the regions of Judea and Samaria, except the apostles.

2 And devout men carried Stephen *to his burial,* and made great lamentation over him.

3 As for Saul, he made havoc of the church, entering every house, and dragging off men and women, committing *them* to prison.

4 Therefore those who were scattered went everywhere preaching the word.

5 Then Philip went down to the city of Samaria and preached Christ to them.

6 And the multitudes with one accord heeded the things spoken by Philip, hearing and seeing the miracles which he did.

7 For unclean spirits, crying with a loud voice, came out of many who were possessed; and many who

were paralyzed and lame were healed.

8 And there was great joy in that city.

9 But there was a certain man called Simon, who previously practiced sorcery in the city and astonished the people of Samaria, claiming that he was someone great,

10 to whom they all gave heed, from the least to the greatest, saying, "This man is the great power of God."

11 And they heeded him because he had astonished them with his sorceries for a long time.

12 But when they believed Philip as he preached the things concerning the kingdom of God and the name of Jesus Christ, both men and women were baptized.

13 Then Simon himself also believed; and when he was baptized he continued with Philip, and was amazed, seeing the miracles and signs which were done.

14 Now when the apostles who were at Jerusalem heard that Samaria had received the word of God, they sent Peter and John to them,

15 who, when they had come down, prayed for them that they might receive the Holy Spirit.

16 For as yet He had fallen upon none of them. They had only been baptized in the name of the Lord Jesus.

17 Then they laid hands on them, and they received the Holy Spirit.

18 Now when Simon saw that through the laying on of the apostles' hands the Holy Spirit was given, he offered them money,

19 saying, "Give me this power also, that anyone on whom I lay hands may receive the Holy Spirit."

20 But Peter said to him, "Your money perish with you, because you thought that the gift of God could be purchased with money!

21 "You have neither part nor portion in this matter, for your heart is not right in the sight of God.

22 "Repent therefore of this your wickedness, and

pray God if perhaps the thought of your heart may be forgiven you.

23 "For I see that you are poisoned by bitterness and bound by iniquity."

24 Then Simon answered and said, "Pray to the Lord for me, that none of the things which you have spoken may come upon me."

25 So when they had testified and preached the word of the Lord, they returned to Jerusalem, preaching the gospel in many villages of the Samaritans.

26 Now an angel of the Lord spoke to Philip, saying, "Arise and go toward the south along the road which goes down from Jerusalem to Gaza." This is desert.

27 So he arose and went. And behold, a man of Ethiopia, a eunuch of great authority under Candace the queen of the Ethiopians, who had charge of all her treasury, and had come to Jerusalem to worship,

28 was returning. And sitting in his chariot, he was reading Isaiah the prophet.

29 Then the Spirit said to Philip, "Go near and overtake this chariot."

30 So Philip ran to him, and heard him reading the prophet Isaiah, and said, "Do you understand what you are reading?"

31 And he said, "How can I, unless someone guides me?" And he asked Philip to come up and sit with him.

32 The place in the Scripture which he read was this: *"He was led as a sheep to the slaughter; and like a lamb silent before its shearer, so He opened not His mouth.*

33 *"In His humiliation His justice was taken away. And who will declare His generation? For His life is taken from the earth."*

34 So the eunuch answered Philip and said, "I ask you, of whom does the prophet say this, of himself or of some other man?"

35 Then Philip opened his mouth, and beginning

at this Scripture, preached Jesus to him.

36 Now as they went down the road, they came to some water. And the eunuch said, "See, *here is* water. What hinders me from being baptized?"

37 Then Philip said, "If you believe with all your heart, you may." And he answered and said, "I believe that Jesus Christ is the Son of God."

38 So he commanded the chariot to stand still. And both Philip and the eunuch went down into the water, and he baptized him.

39 Now when they came up out of the water, the Spirit of the Lord caught Philip away, so that the eunuch saw him no more; and he went on his way rejoicing.

40 But Philip was found at Azotus. And passing through, he preached in all the cities till he came to Caesarea.

ACTS 9

Then Saul, still breathing threats and murder against the disciples of the Lord, went to the high priest

2 and asked letters from him to the synagogues of Damascus, so that if he found any who were of the Way, whether men or women, he might bring them bound to Jerusalem.

3 And as he journeyed he came near Damascus, and suddenly a light shone around him from heaven.

4 Then he fell to the ground, and heard a voice saying to him, "Saul, Saul, why are you persecuting Me?"

5 And he said, "Who are You, Lord?" And the Lord said, "I am Jesus, whom you are persecuting. *It is* hard for you to kick against the goads."

6 So he, trembling and astonished, said, "Lord, what do You want me to do?" And the Lord *said* to him, "Arise and go into the city, and you will be told what you must do."

7 And the men who journeyed with him stood speechless, hearing a voice but seeing no one.

8 Then Saul arose from the ground, and when his eyes were opened he saw no one. But they led him by the hand and brought *him* into Damascus.

9 And he was three days without sight, and neither ate nor drank.

10 Now there was a certain disciple at Damascus named Ananias; and to him the Lord said in a vision, "Ananias." And he said, "Here I am, Lord."

11 So the Lord *said* to him, "Arise and go to the street called Straight, and inquire at the house of Judas for *one* called Saul of Tarsus, for behold, he is praying.

12 "And in a vision he has seen a man named Ananias coming in and putting *his* hand on him, so that he might receive his sight."

13 Then Ananias answered, "Lord, I have heard from many about this man, how much harm he has done to Your saints in Jerusalem.

14 "And here he has authority from the chief priests to bind all who call on Your name."

15 But the Lord said to him, "Go, for he is a chosen vessel of Mine to bear My name before Gentiles, kings, and the children of Israel.

16 "For I will show him how many things he must suffer for My name's sake."

17 And Ananias went his way and entered the house; and laying his hands on him he said, "Brother Saul, the Lord Jesus, who appeared to you on the road as you came, has sent me that you may receive your sight and be filled with the Holy Spirit."

18 Immediately there fell from his eyes *something* like scales, and he received his sight at once; and he arose and was baptized.

19 And when he had received food, he was strengthened. Then Saul spent some days with the disciples at Damascus.

20 Immediately he preached the Christ in the synagogues, that He is the Son of God.

21 Then all who heard were amazed, and said, "Is this not he who destroyed those who called on this name in Jerusalem, and has come here for that purpose, so that he might bring them bound to the chief priests?"

22 But Saul increased all the more in strength, and confounded the Jews who dwelt in Damascus, proving that this *Jesus* is the Christ.

23 Now after many days were past, the Jews plotted to kill him.

24 But their plot became known to Saul. And they watched the gates day and night, to kill him.

25 Then the disciples took him by night and let *him* down through the wall in a large basket.

26 And when Saul had come to Jerusalem, he tried to join the disciples; but they were all afraid of him, and did not believe that he was a disciple.

27 But Barnabas took him and brought *him* to the apostles. And he declared to them how he had seen the Lord on the road, and that He had spoken to him, and how he had preached boldly at Damascus in the name of Jesus.

28 So he was with them at Jerusalem, coming in and going out.

29 And he spoke boldly in the name of the Lord Jesus and disputed against the Hellenists, but they attempted to kill him.

30 When the brethren found out, they brought him down to Caesarea and sent him out to Tarsus.

31 Then the churches throughout all Judea, Galilee, and Samaria had peace and were edified. And walking in the fear of the Lord and in the comfort of the Holy Spirit, they were multiplied.

32 Now it came to pass, as Peter went through all *parts of the country,* that he also came down to the saints who dwelt in Lydda.

33 There he found a certain man named Aeneas, who had been bedridden eight years and was paralyzed.

34 And Peter said to him, "Aeneas, Jesus the Christ heals you. Arise and make your bed." Then he arose immediately.

35 So all who dwelt at Lydda and Sharon saw him and turned to the Lord.

36 At Joppa there was a certain disciple named Tabitha, which is translated Dorcas. This woman was full of good works and charitable deeds which she did.

37 But it happened in those days that she became sick and died. When they had washed her, they laid *her* in an upper room.

38 And since Lydda was near Joppa, and the disciples had heard that Peter was there, they sent two men to him, imploring *him* not to delay in coming to them .

39 Then Peter arose and went with them. When he had come, they brought *him* to the upper room. And all the widows stood by him weeping, showing the tunics and garments which Dorcas had made while she was with them.

40 But Peter put them all out, and knelt down and prayed. And turning to the body he said, "Tabitha, arise." And she opened her eyes, and when she saw Peter she sat up.

41 Then he gave her *his* hand and lifted her up; and when he had called the saints and widows, he presented her alive.

42 And it became known throughout all Joppa, and many believed on the Lord.

43 So it was that he stayed many days in Joppa with Simon, a tanner.

ACTS 10

There was a certain man in Caesarea called Cornelius, a centurion of what was called the Italian Regiment,

2 a devout *man* and one who feared God with all his household, who gave alms generously to the people, and prayed to God always.

3 About the ninth hour of the day he saw clearly in a vision an angel of God coming in and saying to him, "Cornelius!"

4 And when he observed him, he was afraid, and said, "What is it, lord?" So he said to him, "Your prayers and your alms have come up for a memorial before God.

5 "Now send men to Joppa, and send for Simon whose surname is Peter.

6 "He is lodging with Simon, a tanner, whose house is by the sea. He will tell you what you must do."

7 And when the angel who spoke to him had departed, Cornelius called two of his household servants and a devout soldier from among those who waited on him continually.

8 So when he had explained all *these* things to them, he sent them to Joppa.

9 The next day, as they went on their journey and drew near the city, Peter went up on the housetop to pray, about the sixth hour.

10 Then he became very hungry and wanted to eat; but while they made ready, he fell into a trance

11 and saw heaven opened and an object like a great sheet bound at the four corners, descending to him and let down to the earth.

12 In it were all kinds of four-footed animals of the earth, wild beasts, creeping things, and birds of the air.

13 And a voice came to him, "Rise, Peter; kill and eat."

14 But Peter said, "Not so, Lord! For I have never eaten anything common or unclean."

15 And a voice *spoke* to him again the second time, "What God has cleansed you must not call common."

16 This was done three times. And the object was taken up into heaven again.

17 Now while Peter wondered within himself what this vision which he had seen meant, behold, the men who had been sent from Cornelius had made inquiry for Simon's house, and stood before the gate.

18 And they called and asked whether Simon, whose surname was Peter, was lodging there.

19 While Peter thought about the vision, the Spirit said to him, "Behold, three men are seeking you.

20 "Arise therefore, go down and go with them, doubting nothing; for I have sent them."

21 Then Peter went down to the men who had been sent to him from Cornelius, and said, "Yes, I am he whom you seek. For what reason have you come?"

22 And they said, "Cornelius *the* centurion, a just man, one who fears God and has a good reputation among all the nation of the Jews, was divinely instructed by a holy angel to summon you to his house, and to hear words from you."

23 Then he invited them in and lodged *them*. On the next day Peter went away with them, and some brethren from Joppa accompanied him.

24 And the following day they entered Caesarea. Now Cornelius was waiting for them, and had called together his relatives and close friends.

25 As Peter was coming in, Cornelius met him and fell down at his feet and worshiped *him*.

26 But Peter lifted him up, saying, "Stand up; I myself am also a man."

27 And as he talked with him, he went in and found many who had come together.

28 Then he said to them, "You know how unlawful it is for a Jewish man to keep company with or go to one of another nation. But God has shown me that I should not call any man common or unclean.

29 "Therefore I came without objection as soon as I was sent for. I ask, then, for what reason have you sent for me?"

30 And Cornelius said, "Four days ago I was fasting until this hour; and at the ninth hour I prayed in my house, and behold, a man stood before me in bright clothing,

31 "and said, 'Cornelius, your prayer has been heard, and your alms are remembered in the sight of God.

32 'Send therefore to Joppa and call Simon here, whose surname is Peter. He is lodging in the house of Simon, a tanner, by the sea. When he comes, he will speak to you.'

33 "So I sent to you immediately, and you have done well to come. Now therefore, we are all present before God, to hear all the things commanded you by God."

34 Then Peter opened *his* mouth and said: "In truth I perceive that God shows no partiality.

35 "But in every nation whoever fears Him and works righteousness is accepted by Him.

36 "The word which *God* sent to the children of Israel, preaching peace through Jesus Christ — He is Lord of all —

37 "that word you know, which was proclaimed throughout all Judea, and began from Galilee after the baptism which John preached:

38 "how God anointed Jesus of Nazareth with the Holy Spirit and with power, who went about doing good and healing all who were oppressed by the devil, for God was with Him.

39 "And we are witnesses of all things which He did both in the land of the Jews and in Jerusalem, whom they killed by hanging on a tree.

40 "Him God raised up on the third day, and showed Him openly,

41 "not to all the people, but to witnesses chosen before by God, *even* to us who ate and drank with Him after He arose from the dead.

42 "And He commanded us to preach to the people, and to testify that it is He who was ordained by God *to be* Judge of the living and the dead.

43 "To Him all the prophets witness that, through His name, whoever believes in Him will receive remission of sins."

44 While Peter was still speaking these words, the Holy Spirit fell upon all those who heard the word.

45 And those of the circumcision who believed

were astonished, as many as came with Peter, because the gift of the Holy Spirit had been poured out on the Gentiles also.

46 For they heard them speak with tongues and magnify God. Then Peter answered,

47 "Can anyone forbid water, that these should not be baptized who have received the Holy Spirit just as we *have?*"

48 And he commanded them to be baptized in the name of the Lord. Then they asked him to stay a few days.

ACTS 11

N ow the apostles and brethren who were in Judea heard that the Gentiles had also received the word of God.

2 And when Peter came up to Jerusalem, those of the circumcision contended with him,

3 saying, "You went in to uncircumcised men and ate with them!"

4 But Peter explained *it* to them in order from the beginning, saying:

5 "I was in the city of Joppa praying; and in a trance I saw a vision, an object descending like a great sheet, let down from heaven by four corners; and it came to me.

6 "When I observed it intently and considered, I saw four-footed animals of the earth, wild beasts, creeping things, and birds of the air.

7 "And I heard a voice saying to me, 'Rise, Peter; kill and eat.'

8 "But I said, 'Not so, Lord! For nothing common or unclean has at any time entered my mouth.'

9 "But the voice answered me again from heaven, 'What God has cleansed you must not call common.'

10 "Now this was done three times, and all were drawn up again into heaven.

11 "At that very moment, three men stood before

the house where I was, having been sent to me from Caesarea.

12 "Then the Spirit told me to go with them, doubting nothing. Moreover these six brethren accompanied me, and we entered the man's house.

13 "And he told us how he had seen an angel standing in his house, who said to him, 'Send men to Joppa, and call for Simon whose surname is Peter,

14 'who will tell you words by which you and all your household will be saved.'

15 "And as I began to speak, the Holy Spirit fell upon them, as upon us at the beginning.

16 "Then I remembered the word of the Lord, how He said, 'John indeed baptized with water, but you shall be baptized with the Holy Spirit.'

17 "If therefore God gave them the same gift as *He gave* us when we believed on the Lord Jesus Christ, who was I that I could withstand God?"

18 When they heard these things they became silent; and they glorified God, saying, "Then God has also granted to the Gentiles repentance to life."

19 Now those who were scattered after the persecution that arose over Stephen traveled as far as Phoenicia, Cyprus, and Antioch, preaching the word to no one but the Jews only.

20 But some of them were men from Cyprus and Cyrene, who, when they had come to Antioch, spoke to the Hellenists, preaching the Lord Jesus.

21 And the hand of the Lord was with them, and a great number believed and turned to the Lord.

22 Then news of these things came to the ears of the church in Jerusalem, and they sent out Barnabas to go as far as Antioch.

23 When he came and had seen the grace of God, he was glad, and encouraged them all that with purpose of heart they should continue with the Lord.

24 For he was a good man, full of the Holy Spirit and of faith. And a great many people were added to the Lord.

25 Then Barnabas departed for Tarsus to seek Saul.

26 And when he had found him, he brought him to Antioch. So it was that for a whole year they assembled with the church and taught a great many people. And the disciples were first called Christians in Antioch.

27 And in these days prophets came from Jerusalem to Antioch.

28 Then one of them, named Agabus, stood up and showed by the Spirit that there was going to be a great famine throughout all the world, which also happened in the days of Claudius Caesar.

29 Then the disciples, each according to his ability, determined to send relief to the brethren dwelling in Judea.

30 This they also did, and sent it to the elders by the hands of Barnabas and Saul.

ACTS 12

N ow about that time Herod the king stretched out *his* hand to harass some from the church.

2 Then he killed James the brother of John with the sword.

3 And because he saw that it pleased the Jews, he proceeded further to seize Peter also. Now it was *during* the Days of Unleavened Bread.

4 So when he had apprehended him, he put *him* in prison, and delivered *him* to four squads of soldiers to keep him, intending to bring him before the people after Passover.

5 Peter was therefore kept in prison, but constant prayer was offered to God for him by the church.

6 And when Herod was about to bring him out, that night Peter was sleeping, bound with two chains between two soldiers; and the guards before the door were keeping the prison.

7 Now behold, an angel of the Lord stood by *him,* and a light shone in the prison; and he struck Peter on the side and raised him up, saying, "Arise quickly!" And his chains fell off *his* hands.

8 Then the angel said to him, "Gird yourself and tie on your sandals"; and so he did. And he said to him, "Put on your garment and follow me."

9 So he went out and followed him, and did not know that what was done by the angel was real, but thought he was seeing a vision.

10 When they were past the first and the second guard posts, they came to the iron gate that leads to the city, which opened to them of its own accord; and they went out and went down one street, and immediately the angel departed from him.

11 And when Peter had come to himself, he said, "Now I know for certain that the Lord has sent His angel, and has delivered me from the hand of Herod and *from* all the expectation of the Jewish people."

12 So, when he had considered *this,* he came to the house of Mary, the mother of John whose surname was Mark, where many were gathered together praying.

13 And as Peter knocked at the door of the gate, a girl named Rhoda came to answer.

14 When she recognized Peter's voice, because of *her* gladness she did not open the gate, but ran in and announced that Peter stood before the gate.

15 But they said to her, "You are beside yourself!" Yet she kept insisting that it was so. So they said, "It is his angel."

16 Now Peter continued knocking; and when they opened *the door* and saw him, they were astonished.

17 But motioning to them with his hand to keep silent, he declared to them how the Lord had brought him out of the prison. And he said, "Go, tell these things to James and to the brethren." And he departed and went to another place.

18 Then, as soon as it was day, there was no small stir among the soldiers about what had become of Peter.

19 But when Herod had searched for him and not found him, he examined the guards and commanded that *they* should be put to death. And he went down from Judea to Caesarea, and stayed *there*.

20 Now Herod had been very angry with the people of Tyre and Sidon; but they came to him with one accord, and having made Blastus the king's chamberlain their friend, they asked for peace, because their country was supplied with food by the king's *country*.

21 So on a set day Herod, arrayed in royal apparel, sat on his throne and gave an oration to them.

22 And the people kept shouting, "The voice of a god and not of a man!"

23 Then immediately an angel of the Lord struck him, because he did not give glory to God. And he was eaten by worms and died.

24 But the word of God grew and multiplied.

25 And Barnabas and Saul returned from Jerusalem when they had fulfilled *their* ministry, and they also took with them John whose surname was Mark.

ACTS 13

Now in the church that was at Antioch there were certain prophets and teachers: Barnabas, Simeon who was called Niger, Lucius of Cyrene, Manaen who had been brought up with Herod the tetrarch, and Saul.

2 As they ministered to the Lord and fasted, the Holy Spirit said, "Now separate to Me Barnabas and Saul for the work to which I have called them."

3 Then, having fasted and prayed, and laid hands on them, they sent *them* away.

4 So, being sent out by the Holy Spirit, they went down to Seleucia, and from there they sailed to Cyprus.

5 And when they arrived in Salamis, they preached the word of God in the synagogues of the Jews. They also had John as *their* assistant.

6 Now when they had gone through the island to Paphos, they found a certain sorcerer, a false prophet, a Jew whose name *was* Bar-Jesus,

7 who was with the proconsul, Sergius Paulus, an intelligent man. This man called for Barnabas and Saul and sought to hear the word of God.

8 But Elymas the sorcerer (for so his name is translated) withstood them, seeking to turn the proconsul away from the faith.

9 Then Saul, who also *is called* Paul, filled with the Holy Spirit, looked intently at him

10 and said, "O full of all deceit and all fraud, *you* son of the devil, *you* enemy of all righteousness, will you not cease perverting the straight ways of the Lord?

11 "And now, indeed, the hand of the Lord *is* upon you, and you shall be blind, not seeing the sun for a time." And immediately a dark mist fell on him, and he went around seeking someone to lead him by the hand.

12 Then the proconsul believed, when he saw what had been done, being astonished at the teaching of the Lord.

13 Now when Paul and his party set sail from Paphos, they came to Perga in Pamphylia; and John, departing from them, returned to Jerusalem.

14 But when they departed from Perga, they came to Antioch in Pisidia, and went into the synagogue on the Sabbath day and sat down.

15 And after the reading of the Law and the Prophets, the rulers of the synagogue sent to them, saying, "Men *and* brethren, if you have any word of exhortation for the people, say on."

16 Then Paul stood up, and motioning with *his* hand said, "Men of Israel, and you who fear God, listen:

17 "The God of this people Israel chose our fathers, and exalted the people when they dwelt as strangers in the land of Egypt, and with an uplifted arm He brought them out of it.

18 "Now for a time of about forty years He put up

with their ways in the wilderness.

19 "And when He had destroyed seven nations in the land of Canaan, He distributed their land to them by allotment.

20 "After that He gave *them* judges for about four hundred and fifty years, until Samuel the prophet.

21 "And afterward they asked for a king; so God gave them Saul the son of Kish, a man of the tribe of Benjamin, for forty years.

22 "And when He had removed him, He raised up for them David as king, to whom also He gave testimony and said, '*I have found David* the son of Jesse, *a man after My own heart*, who will do all My will.'

23 "From this man's seed, according to *the* promise, God raised up for Israel a Savior — Jesus —

24 "after John had first preached, before His coming, the baptism of repentance to all the people of Israel.

25 "And as John was finishing his course, he said, 'Who do you think I am? I am not *He*. But behold, there comes One after me, the sandals of whose feet I am not worthy to loose.'

26 "Men *and* brethren, sons of the family of Abraham, and those among you who fear God, to you the word of this salvation has been sent.

27 "For those who dwell in Jerusalem, and their rulers, because they did not know Him, nor even the voices of the Prophets which are read every Sabbath, have fulfilled *them* in condemning *Him*.

28 "And though they found no cause for death *in Him,* they asked Pilate that He should be put to death.

29 "Now when they had fulfilled all that was written concerning Him, they took *Him* down from the tree and laid *Him* in a tomb.

30 "But God raised Him from the dead.

31 "He was seen for many days by those who came up with Him from Galilee to Jerusalem, who are His witnesses to the people.

32 "And we declare to you glad tidings — that

promise which was made to the fathers.

33 "God has fulfilled this for us their children, in that He has raised up Jesus. As it is also written in the second Psalm: 'You are My Son, today I have begotten You.'

34 "And that He raised Him from the dead, no more to return to corruption, He has spoken thus: 'I will give you the sure mercies of David.'

35 "Therefore He also says in another *Psalm:* 'You will not allow Your Holy One to see corruption.'

36 "For David, after he had served his own generation by the will of God, fell asleep, was buried with his fathers, and saw corruption;

37 "but He whom God raised up saw no corruption.

38 "Therefore let it be known to you, brethren, that through this Man is preached to you the forgiveness of sins;

39 "and by Him everyone who believes is justified from all things from which you could not be justified by the law of Moses.

40 "Beware therefore, lest what has been spoken in the prophets come upon you:

41 'Behold, you despisers, marvel and perish; for I work a work in your days, a work which you will by no means believe, though one were to declare it to you.' "

42 And when the Jews went out of the synagogue, the Gentiles begged that these words might be preached to them the next Sabbath.

43 Now when the congregation had broken up, many of the Jews and devout proselytes followed Paul and Barnabas, who, speaking to them, persuaded them to continue in the grace of God.

44 And the next Sabbath almost the whole city came together to hear the word of God.

45 But when the Jews saw the multitudes, they were filled with envy; and contradicting and blaspheming, they opposed the things spoken by Paul.

46 Then Paul and Barnabas grew bold and said, "It was necessary that the word of God should be spoken to you first; but since you reject it, and judge yourselves unworthy of everlasting life, behold, we turn to the Gentiles.

47 "For so the Lord has commanded us: *'I have set you to be a light to the Gentiles, that you should be for salvation to the ends of the earth.'* "

48 Now when the Gentiles heard this, they were glad and glorified the word of the Lord. And as many as had been appointed to eternal life believed.

49 And the word of the Lord was being spread throughout all the region.

50 But the Jews stirred up the devout and prominent women and the chief men of the city, raised up persecution against Paul and Barnabas, and expelled them from their region.

51 But they shook off the dust from their feet against them, and came to Iconium.

52 And the disciples were filled with joy and with the Holy Spirit.

ACTS 14

Now it happened in Iconium that they went together to the synagogue of the Jews, and so spoke that a great multitude both of the Jews and of the Greeks believed.

2 But the unbelieving Jews stirred up the Gentiles and poisoned their minds against the brethren.

3 Therefore they stayed there a long time, speaking boldly in the Lord, who was bearing witness to the word of His grace, granting signs and wonders to be done by their hands.

4 But the multitude of the city was divided: part sided with the Jews, and part with the apostles.

5 And when a violent attempt was made by both the Gentiles and Jews, with their rulers, to abuse and

stone them,

6 they became aware of it and fled to Lystra and Derbe, cities of Lycaonia, and to the surrounding region.

7 And they were preaching the gospel there.

8 And in Lystra a certain man without strength in his feet was sitting, a cripple from his mother's womb, who had never walked.

9 *This* man heard Paul speaking. Paul, observing him intently and seeing that he had faith to be healed,

10 said with a loud voice, "Stand up straight on your feet!" And he leaped and walked.

11 Now when the people saw what Paul had done, they raised their voices, saying in the Lycaonian *language,* "The gods have come down to us in the likeness of men!"

12 And Barnabas they called Zeus, and Paul, Hermes, because he was the chief speaker.

13 Then the priest of Zeus, whose temple was in front of their city, brought oxen and garlands to the gates, intending to sacrifice with the multitudes.

14 But when the apostles Barnabas and Paul heard this, they tore their clothes and ran in among the multitude, crying out

15 and saying, "Men, why are you doing these things? We also are men with the same nature as you, and preach to you that you should turn from these vain things to the living God, who made the heaven, the earth, the sea, and all things that are in them,

16 "who in bygone generations allowed all nations to walk in their own ways.

17 "Nevertheless He did not leave Himself without witness, in that He did good, gave us rain from heaven and fruitful seasons, filling our hearts with food and gladness."

18 And with these sayings they could scarcely restrain the multitudes from sacrificing to them.

19 Then Jews from Antioch and Iconium came there; and having persuaded the multitudes, they

stoned Paul *and* dragged *him* out of the city, supposing him to be dead.

20 However, when the disciples gathered around him, he rose up and went into the city. And the next day he departed with Barnabas to Derbe.

21 And when they had preached the gospel to that city and made many disciples, they returned to Lystra, Iconium, and Antioch,

22 strengthening the souls of the disciples, exhorting *them* to continue in the faith, and *saying,* "We must through many tribulations enter the kingdom of God."

23 So when they had appointed elders in every church, and prayed with fasting, they commended them to the Lord in whom they had believed.

24 And after they had passed through Pisidia, they came to Pamphylia.

25 Now when they had preached the word in Perga, they went down to Attalia.

26 From there they sailed to Antioch, where they had been commended to the grace of God for the work which they had completed.

27 And when they had come and gathered the church together, they reported all that God had done with them, and that He had opened the door of faith to the Gentiles.

28 So they stayed there a long time with the disciples.

ACTS 15

And certain *men* came down from Judea and taught the brethren, "Unless you are circumcised according to the custom of Moses, you cannot be saved."

2 Therefore, when Paul and Barnabas had no small dissension and dispute with them, they determined that Paul and Barnabas and certain others of them should go up to Jerusalem, to the apostles and elders, about this question.

3 So, being sent on their way by the church, they passed through Phoenicia and Samaria, describing the conversion of the Gentiles; and they caused great joy to all the brethren.

4 And when they had come to Jerusalem, they were received by the church and the apostles and the elders; and they reported all things that God had done with them.

5 But some of the sect of the Pharisees who believed rose up, saying, "It is necessary to circumcise them, and to command *them* to keep the law of Moses."

6 So the apostles and elders came together to consider this matter.

7 And when there had been much dispute, Peter rose up and said to them: "Men and brethren, you know that a good while ago God chose among us, that by my mouth the Gentiles should hear the word of the gospel and believe.

8 "So God, who knows the heart, acknowledged them, by giving them the Holy Spirit just as *He did* to us,

9 "and made no distinction between us and them, purifying their hearts by faith.

10 "Now therefore, why do you test God by putting a yoke on the neck of the disciples which neither our fathers nor we were able to bear?

11 "But we believe that through the grace of the Lord Jesus Christ we shall be saved in the same manner as they."

12 Then all the multitude kept silent and listened to Barnabas and Paul declaring how many miracles and wonders God had worked through them among the Gentiles.

13 And after they had become silent, James answered, saying, "Men *and* brethren, listen to me:

14 "Simon has declared how God at the first visited the Gentiles to take out of them a people for His name.

15 "And with this the words of the prophets agree, just as it is written:

16 'After this I will return and will rebuild the tabernacle of David which has fallen down. I will rebuild its ruins, and I will set it up,

17 'so that the rest of mankind may seek the Lord, even all the Gentiles who are called by My name, Says the Lord who does all these things.'

18 "Known to God from eternity are all His works.

19 "Therefore I judge that we should not trouble those from among the Gentiles who are turning to God,

20 "but that we write to them to abstain from things polluted by idols, *from* sexual immorality, *from* things strangled, and *from* blood.

21 "For Moses has had throughout many generations those who preach him in every city, being read in the synagogues every Sabbath."

22 Then it pleased the apostles and elders, with the whole church, to send chosen men of their own company to Antioch with Paul and Barnabas, *namely,* Judas who was also named Barsabas, and Silas, leading men among the brethren.

23 They wrote this *letter* by them: The apostles, the elders, and the brethren, to the brethren who are of the Gentiles in Antioch, Syria, and Cilicia: Greetings.

24 Since we have heard that some who went out from us have troubled you with words, unsettling your souls, saying, *'You must* be circumcised and keep the law' — to whom we gave no *such* commandment —

25 it seemed good to us, being assembled with one accord, to send chosen men to you with our beloved Barnabas and Paul,

26 men who have risked their lives for the name of our Lord Jesus Christ.

27 We have therefore sent Judas and Silas, who will also report the same things by word of mouth.

28 For it seemed good to the Holy Spirit, and to us, to lay upon you no greater burden than these necessary things:

29 that you abstain from things offered to idols,

from blood, from things strangled, and from sexual immorality. If you keep yourselves from these, you will do well. Farewell.

30 So when they were sent off, they came to Antioch; and when they had gathered the multitude together, they delivered the letter.

31 When they had read it, they rejoiced over its encouragement.

32 Now Judas and Silas, themselves being prophets also, exhorted the brethren with many words and strengthened *them*.

33 And after they had stayed *there* for a time, they were sent back with greetings from the brethren to the apostles.

34 However, it seemed good to Silas to remain there.

35 Paul and Barnabas also remained in Antioch, teaching and preaching the word of the Lord, with many others also.

36 Then after some days Paul said to Barnabas, "Let us now go back and visit our brethren in every city where we have preached the word of the Lord, *and see* how they are doing."

37 Now Barnabas was determined to take with them John called Mark.

38 But Paul insisted that they should not take with them the one who had departed from them in Pamphylia, and had not gone with them to the work.

39 Then the contention became so sharp that they parted from one another. And so Barnabas took Mark and sailed to Cyprus;

40 but Paul chose Silas and departed, being commended by the brethren to the grace of God.

41 And he went through Syria and Cilicia, strengthening the churches.

ACTS 16

Then he came to Derbe and Lystra. And behold, a certain disciple was there, named Timothy, *the* son of a certain Jewish woman who believed, but his father *was* Greek.

2 He was well spoken of by the brethren who were at Lystra and Iconium.

3 Paul wanted to have him go on with him. And he took *him* and circumcised him because of the Jews who were in that region, for they all knew that his father was Greek.

4 And as they went through the cities, they delivered to them the decrees to keep, which were determined by the apostles and elders at Jerusalem.

5 So the churches were strengthened in the faith, and increased in number daily .

6 Now when they had gone through Phrygia and the region of Galatia, they were forbidden by the Holy Spirit to preach the word in Asia.

7 After they had come to Mysia, they tried to go into Bithynia, but the Spirit did not permit them.

8 So passing by Mysia, they came down to Troas.

9 And a vision appeared to Paul in the night. A man of Macedonia stood and pleaded with him, saying, "Come over to Macedonia and help us."

10 Now after he had seen the vision, immediately we sought to go to Macedonia, concluding that the Lord had called us to preach the gospel to them.

11 Therefore, sailing from Troas, we ran a straight course to Samothrace, and the next *day* came to Neapolis,

12 and from there to Philippi, which is the foremost city of that part of Macedonia, a colony. And we were staying in that city for some days.

13 And on the Sabbath day we went out of the city to the riverside, where prayer was customarily made; and we sat down and spoke to the women who met *there*.

14 Now a certain woman named Lydia heard *us*. She was a seller of purple from the city of Thyatira, who worshiped God. The Lord opened her heart to heed the things spoken by Paul.

15 And when she and her household were baptized, she begged *us*, saying, "If you have judged me to be faithful to the Lord, come to my house and stay." And she constrained us.

16 Now it happened, as we went to prayer, that a certain slave girl possessed with a spirit of divination met us, who brought her masters much profit by fortune-telling.

17 This girl followed Paul and us, and cried out, saying, "These men are the servants of the Most High God, who proclaim to us the way of salvation."

18 And this she did for many days. But Paul, greatly annoyed, turned and said to the spirit, "I command you in the name of Jesus Christ to come out of her." And he came out that very hour.

19 But when her masters saw that their hope of profit was gone, they seized Paul and Silas and dragged *them* into the marketplace to the authorities.

20 And they brought them to the magistrates, and said, "These men, being Jews, exceedingly trouble our city;

21 "and they teach customs which are not lawful for us, being Romans, to receive or observe."

22 Then the multitude rose up together against them; and the magistrates tore off their clothes and commanded *them* to be beaten with rods.

23 And when they had laid many stripes on them, they threw *them* into prison, commanding the jailer to keep them securely.

24 Having received such a charge, he put them into the inner prison and fastened their feet in the stocks.

25 But at midnight Paul and Silas were praying and singing hymns to God, and the prisoners were listening to them.

26 Suddenly there was a great earthquake, so that the foundations of the prison were shaken; and immediately all the doors were opened and everyone's chains were loosed.

27 And the keeper of the prison, awaking from sleep and seeing the prison doors open, supposing the prisoners had fled, drew his sword and was about to kill himself.

28 But Paul called with a loud voice, saying, "Do yourself no harm, for we are all here."

29 Then he called for a light, ran in, and fell down trembling before Paul and Silas.

30 And he brought them out and said, "Sirs, what must I do to be saved?"

31 So they said, "Believe on the Lord Jesus Christ, and you will be saved, you and your household."

32 Then they spoke the word of the Lord to him and to all who were in his house.

33 And he took them the same hour of the night and washed *their* stripes. And immediately he and all his family were baptized.

34 Now when he had brought them into his house, he set food before them; and he rejoiced, having believed in God with all his household.

35 And when it was day, the magistrates sent the officers, saying, "Let those men go."

36 So the keeper of the prison reported these words to Paul, saying, "The magistrates have sent to let you go. Now therefore depart, and go in peace."

37 But Paul said to them, "They have beaten us openly, uncondemned Romans, *and* have thrown *us* into prison. And now do they put us out secretly? No indeed! Let them come themselves and get us out."

38 And the officers told these words to the magistrates, and they were afraid when they heard that they were Romans.

39 Then they came and pleaded with them and brought *them* out, and asked *them* to depart from the city.

40 So they went out of the prison and entered *the house of* Lydia; and when they had seen the brethren, they encouraged them and departed.

ACTS 17

Now when they had passed through Amphipolis and Apollonia, they came to Thessalonica, where there was a synagogue of the Jews.

2 Then Paul, as his custom was, went in to them, and for three Sabbaths reasoned with them from the Scriptures,

3 explaining and demonstrating that the Christ had to suffer and rise again from the dead, and *saying,* "This Jesus whom I preach to you is the Christ."

4 And some of them were persuaded; and a great multitude of the devout Greeks, and not a few of the leading women, joined Paul and Silas.

5 But the Jews who were not persuaded, becoming envious, took some of the evil men from the marketplace, and gathering a mob, set all the city in an uproar and attacked the house of Jason, and sought to bring them out to the people.

6 But when they did not find them, they dragged Jason and some brethren to the rulers of the city, crying out, "These who have turned the world upside down have come here too.

7 "Jason has harbored them, and these are all acting contrary to the decrees of Caesar, saying there is another king — Jesus."

8 And they troubled the crowd and the rulers of the city when they heard these things.

9 So when they had taken security from Jason and the rest, they let them go.

10 Then the brethren immediately sent Paul and Silas away by night to Berea. When they arrived, they went into the synagogue of the Jews.

11 These were more fair-minded than those in

Thessalonica, in that they received the word with all readiness, and searched the Scriptures daily *to find out* whether these things were so.

12 Therefore many of them believed, and also not a few of the Greeks, prominent women as well as men.

13 But when the Jews from Thessalonica learned that the word of God was preached by Paul at Berea, they came there also and stirred up the crowds.

14 Then immediately the brethren sent Paul away, to go to the sea; but both Silas and Timothy remained there.

15 So those who conducted Paul brought him to Athens; and receiving a command for Silas and Timothy to come to him with all speed, they departed.

16 Now while Paul waited for them at Athens, his spirit was provoked within him when he saw that the city was given over to idols.

17 Therefore he reasoned in the synagogue with the Jews and with the *Gentile* worshipers, and in the marketplace daily with those who happened to be there.

18 Then certain Epicurean and Stoic philosophers encountered him. And some said, "What does this babbler want to say?" Others said, "He seems to be a proclaimer of foreign gods," because he preached to them Jesus and the resurrection.

19 And they took him and brought him to the Areopagus, saying, "May we know what this new doctrine *is* of which you speak?

20 "For you are bringing some strange things to our ears. Therefore we want to know what these things mean."

21 For all the Athenians and the foreigners who were there spent their time in nothing else but either to tell or to hear some new thing.

22 Then Paul stood in the midst of the Areopagus and said, "Men of Athens, I perceive that in all things you are very religious;

23 "for as I was passing through and considering

the objects of your worship, I even found an altar with this inscription: TO THE UNKNOWN GOD. Therefore, the One whom you worship without knowing, Him I proclaim to you:

24 "God, who made the world and everything in it, since He is Lord of heaven and earth, does not dwell in temples made with hands.

25 "Nor is He worshiped with men's hands, as though He needed anything, since He gives to all life, breath, and all things.

26 "And He has made from one blood every nation of men to dwell on all the face of the earth, and has determined their preappointed times and the boundaries of their habitation,

27 "so that they should seek the Lord, in the hope that they might grope for Him and find Him, though He is not far from each one of us;

28 "for in Him we live and move and have our being, as also some of your own poets have said, 'For we are also His offspring.'

29 "Therefore, since we are the offspring of God, we ought not to think that the Divine Nature is like gold or silver or stone, something shaped by art and man's devising.

30 "Truly, these times of ignorance God overlooked, but now commands all men everywhere to repent,

31 "because He has appointed a day on which He will judge the world in righteousness by the Man whom He has ordained. He has given assurance of this to all by raising Him from the dead."

32 And when they heard of the resurrection of the dead, some mocked, while others said, "We will hear you again on this *matter.*"

33 So Paul departed from among them.

34 However, some men joined him and believed, among them Dionysius the Areopagite, a woman named Damaris, and others with them.

ACTS 18

After these things Paul departed from Athens and went to Corinth.

2 And he found a certain Jew named Aquila, born in Pontus, who had recently come from Italy with his wife Priscilla (because Claudius had commanded all the Jews to depart from Rome); and he came to them.

3 So, because he was of the same trade, he stayed with them and worked; for by occupation they were tentmakers.

4 And he reasoned in the synagogue every Sabbath, and persuaded both Jews and Greeks.

5 When Silas and Timothy had come from Macedonia, Paul was constrained by the Spirit, and testified to the Jews *that* Jesus *is* the Christ.

6 But when they opposed him and blasphemed, he shook *his* garments and said to them, "Your blood *be* upon your *own* heads; I *am* clean. From now on I will go to the Gentiles."

7 And he departed from there and entered the house of a certain *man* named Justus, *one* who worshiped God, whose house was next door to the synagogue.

8 Then Crispus, the ruler of the synagogue, believed on the Lord with all his household. And many of the Corinthians, hearing, believed and were baptized.

9 Now the Lord spoke to Paul in the night by a vision, "Do not be afraid, but speak, and do not keep silent;

10 "for I am with you, and no one will attack you to hurt you; for I have many people in this city."

11 And he continued *there* a year and six months, teaching the word of God among them.

12 Now when Gallio was proconsul of Achaia, the Jews with one accord rose up against Paul and brought him to the judgment seat,

13 saying, "This *fellow* persuades men to worship God contrary to the law."

14 And when Paul was about to open *his* mouth, Gallio said to the Jews, "If it were a matter of wrongdoing or wicked crimes, O Jews, there would be reason why I should bear with you.

15 "But if it is a question of words and names and your own law, look *to it* yourselves; for I do not want to be a judge of such *matters.*"

16 And he drove them from the judgment seat.

17 Then all the Greeks took Sosthenes, the ruler of the synagogue, and beat *him* before the judgment seat. But Gallio took no notice of these things.

18 So Paul still remained a good while. Then he took leave of the brethren and sailed for Syria, and Priscilla and Aquila *were* with him. He had *his* hair cut off at Cenchrea, for he had taken a vow.

19 And he came to Ephesus, and left them there; but he himself entered the synagogue and reasoned with the Jews.

20 When they asked *him* to stay a longer time with them, he did not consent,

21 but took leave of them, saying, "I must by all means keep this coming feast in Jerusalem; but I will return again to you, God willing." And he sailed from Ephesus.

22 And when he had landed at Caesarea, and gone up and greeted the church, he went down to Antioch.

23 After he had spent some time *there,* he departed and went over *all* the region of Galatia and Phrygia in order, strengthening all the disciples.

24 Now a certain Jew named Apollos, born at Alexandria, an eloquent man *and* mighty in the Scriptures, came to Ephesus.

25 This man had been instructed in the way of the Lord; and being fervent in spirit, he spoke and taught accurately the things of the Lord, though he knew only the baptism of John.

26 So he began to speak boldly in the synagogue. When Aquila and Priscilla heard him, they took him aside and explained to him the way of God more accurately.

27 And when he desired to cross to Achaia, the brethren wrote, exhorting the disciples to receive him; and when he arrived, he greatly helped those who had believed through grace;

28 for he vigorously refuted the Jews publicly, showing from the Scriptures that Jesus is the Christ.

ACTS 19

And it happened, while Apollos was at Corinth, that Paul, having passed through the upper regions, came to Ephesus. And finding some disciples

2 he said to them, "Did you receive the Holy Spirit when you believed?" And they said to him, "We have not so much as heard whether there is a Holy Spirit."

3 And he said to them, "Into what then were you baptized?" So they said, "Into John's baptism."

4 Then Paul said, "John indeed baptized with a baptism of repentance, saying to the people that they should believe on Him who would come after him, that is, on Christ Jesus."

5 When they heard *this,* they were baptized in the name of the Lord Jesus.

6 And when Paul had laid hands on them, the Holy Spirit came upon them, and they spoke with tongues and prophesied.

7 Now the men were about twelve in all.

8 And he went into the synagogue and spoke boldly for three months, reasoning and persuading concerning the things of the kingdom of God.

9 But when some were hardened and did not believe, but spoke evil of the Way before the multitude, he departed from them and withdrew the disciples, reasoning daily in the school of Tyrannus.

10 And this continued for two years, so that all who dwelt in Asia heard the word of the Lord Jesus, both Jews and Greeks.

11 Now God worked unusual miracles by the hands of Paul,

12 so that even handkerchiefs or aprons were brought from his body to the sick, and the diseases left them and the evil spirits went out of them.

13 Then some of the itinerant Jewish exorcists took it upon themselves to call the name of the Lord Jesus over those who had evil spirits, saying, "We adjure you by the Jesus whom Paul preaches."

14 Also there were seven sons of Sceva, a Jewish chief priest, who did so.

15 And the evil spirit answered and said, "Jesus I know, and Paul I know; but who are you?"

16 Then the man in whom the evil spirit was leaped on them, overpowered them, and prevailed against them, so that they fled out of that house naked and wounded.

17 This became known both to all Jews and Greeks dwelling in Ephesus; and fear fell on them all, and the name of the Lord Jesus was magnified.

18 And many who had believed came confessing and telling their deeds.

19 Also, many of those who had practiced magic brought their books together and burned *them* in the sight of all. And they counted up the value of them, and *it* totaled fifty thousand *pieces* of silver.

20 So the word of the Lord grew mightily and prevailed.

21 When these things were accomplished, Paul purposed in the Spirit, when he had passed through Macedonia and Achaia, to go to Jerusalem, saying, "After I have been there, I must also see Rome."

22 So he sent into Macedonia two of those who ministered to him, Timothy and Erastus, but he himself stayed in Asia for a time.

23 And about that time there arose a great commotion about the Way.

24 For a certain man named Demetrius, a silversmith, who made silver shrines of Diana, brought no small profit to the craftsmen.

25 He called them together with the workers of

similar occupation, and said: "Men, you know that we have our prosperity by this trade.

26 "Moreover you see and hear that not only at Ephesus, but throughout almost all Asia, this Paul has persuaded and turned away many people, saying that they are not gods which are made with hands.

27 "So not only is this trade of ours in danger of falling into disrepute, but also the temple of the great goddess Diana may be despised and her magnificence destroyed, whom all Asia and the world worship."

28 And when they heard *this,* they were full of wrath and cried out, saying, "Great *is* Diana of the Ephesians!"

29 So the whole city was filled with confusion, and rushed into the theater with one accord, having seized Gaius and Aristarchus, Macedonians, Paul's travel companions.

30 And when Paul wanted to go in to the people, the disciples would not allow him.

31 Then some of the officials of Asia, who were his friends, sent to him pleading that he would not venture into the theater.

32 Some therefore cried one thing and some another, for the assembly was confused, and most of them did not know why they had come together.

33 And they drew Alexander out of the multitude, the Jews putting him forward. And Alexander motioned with his hand, and wanted to make his defense to the people.

34 But when they found out that he was a Jew, all with one voice cried out for about two hours, "Great *is* Diana of the Ephesians!"

35 And when the city clerk had quieted the crowd, he said: "Men of Ephesus, what man is there who does not know that the city of the Ephesians is temple guardian of the great goddess Diana, and of the *image* which fell down from Zeus?

36 "Therefore, since these things cannot be denied, you ought to be quiet and do nothing rashly.

37 "For you have brought these men here who are neither robbers of temples nor blasphemers of your goddess.

38 "Therefore, if Demetrius and his fellow craftsmen have a case against anyone, the courts are open and there are proconsuls. Let them bring charges against one another.

39 "But if you have any other inquiry to make, it shall be determined in the lawful assembly.

40 "For we are in danger of being called in question for today's uproar, there being no reason which we may give to account for this disorderly gathering."

41 And when he had said these things, he dismissed the assembly.

ACTS 20

After the uproar had ceased, Paul called the disciples to *him,* embraced *them,* and departed to go to Macedonia.

2 Now when he had gone over that region and encouraged them with many words, he came to Greece

3 and stayed three months. And when the Jews plotted against him as he was about to sail to Syria, he decided to return through Macedonia.

4 And Sopater of Berea accompanied him to Asia — also Aristarchus and Secundus of the Thessalonians, and Gaius of Derbe, and Timothy, and Tychicus and Trophimus of Asia.

5 These men, going ahead, waited for us at Troas.

6 But we sailed away from Philippi after the Days of Unleavened Bread, and in five days joined them at Troas, where we stayed seven days.

7 Now on the first *day* of the week, when the disciples came together to break bread, Paul, ready to depart the next day, spoke to them and continued his message until midnight.

8 There were many lamps in the upper room where they were gathered together.

132

9 And in a window sat a certain young man named Eutychus, who was sinking into a deep sleep. He was overcome by sleep; and as Paul continued speaking, he fell down from the third story and was taken up dead.

10 But Paul went down, fell on him, and embracing *him* said, "Do not trouble yourselves, for his life is in him."

11 Now when he had come up, had broken bread and eaten, and talked a long while, even till daybreak, he departed.

12 And they brought the young man in alive, and they were not a little comforted.

13 Then we went ahead to the ship and sailed to Assos, there intending to take Paul on board; for so he had given orders, intending himself to go on foot.

14 And when he met us at Assos, we took him on board and came to Mitylene.

15 We sailed from there, and the next *day* came opposite Chios; the following *day* we arrived at Samos and stayed at Trogyllium; the next *day* we came to Miletus.

16 For Paul had decided to sail past Ephesus, so that he would not have to spend time in Asia; for he was hurrying to be at Jerusalem, if possible, on the Day of Pentecost.

17 From Miletus he sent to Ephesus and called for the elders of the church.

18 And when they had come to him, he said to them: "You know, from the first day that I came to Asia, in what manner I always lived among you,

19 "serving the Lord with all humility, with many tears and trials which happened to me by the plotting of the Jews;

20 "*and* how I kept back nothing that was helpful, but proclaimed it to you, and taught you publicly and from house to house,

21 "testifying to Jews, and also to Greeks, repentance toward God and faith toward our Lord Jesus Christ.

22 "And see, now I go bound in the spirit to Jerusalem, not knowing the things that will happen to me there,

23 "except that the Holy Spirit testifies in every city, saying that chains and tribulations await me.

24 "But none of these things move me; nor do I count my life dear to myself, so that I may finish my race with joy, and the ministry which I received from the Lord Jesus, to testify to the gospel of the grace of God.

25 "And indeed, now I know that you all, among whom I have gone preaching the kingdom of God, will see my face no more.

26 "Therefore I testify to you this day that I *am* innocent of the blood of all *men*.

27 "For I have not shunned to declare to you the whole counsel of God.

28 "Therefore take heed to yourselves and to all the flock, among which the Holy Spirit has made you overseers, to shepherd the church of God which He purchased with His own blood.

29 "For I know this, that after my departure savage wolves will come in among you, not sparing the flock.

30 "Also from among yourselves men will rise up, speaking perverse things, to draw away the disciples after themselves.

31 "Therefore watch, and remember that for three years I did not cease to warn everyone night and day with tears.

32 "And now, brethren, I commend you to God and to the word of His grace, which is able to build you up and give you an inheritance among all those who are sanctified.

33 "I have coveted no one's silver or gold or apparel.

34 "Yes, you yourselves know that these hands have provided for my necessities, and for those who were with me.

35 "I have shown you in every way, by laboring like this, that you must support the weak. And remember the words of the Lord Jesus, that He said, 'It is more blessed to give than to receive.' "

36 And when he had said these things, he knelt down and prayed with them all.

37 Then they all wept freely, and fell on Paul's neck and kissed him,

38 sorrowing most of all for the words which he spoke, that they would see his face no more. And they accompanied him to the ship.

ACTS 21

Now it came to pass, that when we had departed from them and set sail, running a straight course we came to Cos, the following *day* to Rhodes, and from there to Patara.

2 And finding a ship sailing over to Phoenicia, we went aboard and set sail.

3 When we had sighted Cyprus, we passed it on the left, sailed to Syria, and landed at Tyre; for there the ship was to unload her cargo.

4 And finding disciples, we stayed there seven days. They told Paul through the Spirit not to go up to Jerusalem.

5 When we had come to the end of those days, we departed and went on our way; and they all accompanied us, with wives and children, till *we were* out of the city. And we knelt down on the shore and prayed.

6 When we had taken our leave of one another, we boarded the ship, and they returned home.

7 And when we had finished *our* voyage from Tyre, we came to Ptolemais, greeted the brethren, and stayed with them one day.

8 On the next *day* we who were Paul's companions departed and came to Caesarea, and entered the house of Philip the evangelist, who was *one* of the seven, and

stayed with him.

9 Now this man had four virgin daughters who prophesied.

10 And as we stayed many days, a certain prophet named Agabus came down from Judea.

11 When he had come to us, he took Paul's belt, bound his *own* hands and feet, and said, "Thus says the Holy Spirit, 'So shall the Jews at Jerusalem bind the man who owns this belt, and deliver *him* into the hands of the Gentiles.' "

12 And when we heard these things, both we and those from that place pleaded with him not to go up to Jerusalem.

13 Then Paul answered, "What do you mean by weeping and breaking my heart? For I am ready not only to be bound, but also to die at Jerusalem for the name of the Lord Jesus."

14 So when he would not be persuaded, we ceased, saying, "The will of the Lord be done."

15 And after those days we packed and went up to Jerusalem.

16 Also some of the disciples from Caesarea went with us and brought with them one, Mnason of Cyprus, an early disciple, with whom we were to lodge.

17 And when we had come to Jerusalem, the brethren received us gladly.

18 On the following *day* Paul went in with us to James, and all the elders were present.

19 When he had greeted them, he told in detail those things which God had done among the Gentiles through his ministry.

20 And when they heard *it,* they glorified the Lord. And they said to him, "You see, brother, how many myriads of Jews there are who have believed, and they are all zealous for the law;

21 "but they have been informed about you that you teach all the Jews who are among the Gentiles to forsake Moses, saying that they ought not to circumcise *their* children nor to walk according to the customs.

22 "What then? The assembly must certainly meet, for they will hear that you have come.

23 "Therefore do what we tell you: We have four men who have taken a vow.

24 "Take them and be purified with them, and pay their expenses so that they may shave *their* heads, and that all may know that those things of which they were informed concerning you are nothing, but *that* you yourself also walk orderly and keep the law.

25 "But concerning the Gentiles who believe, we have written *and* decided that they should observe no such thing, except that they should keep themselves from *things* offered to idols, from blood, from things strangled, and from sexual immorality."

26 Then Paul took the men, and the next day, having been purified with them, entered the temple to announce the expiration of the days of purification, at which time an offering should be made for each one of them.

27 And when the seven days were almost ended, the Jews from Asia, seeing him in the temple, stirred up the whole crowd and laid hands on him,

28 crying out, "Men of Israel, help! This is the man who teaches all *men* everywhere against the people, the law, and this place; and furthermore he also brought Greeks into the temple and has defiled this holy place."

29 (For they had previously seen Trophimus the Ephesian with him in the city, whom they supposed that Paul had brought into the temple.)

30 And all the city was disturbed; and the people ran together, seized Paul, and dragged him out of the temple; and immediately the doors were shut.

31 Now as they were seeking to kill him, news came to the commander of the garrison that all Jerusalem was in an uproar.

32 He immediately took soldiers and centurions, and ran down to them. And when they saw the commander and the soldiers, they stopped beating Paul.

33 Then the commander came near and took him,

and commanded *him* to be bound with two chains; and he asked who he was and what he had done.

34 And some among the multitude cried one thing and some another. And when he could not ascertain the truth because of the tumult, he commanded him to be taken into the barracks.

35 And when he reached the stairs, he had to be carried by the soldiers because of the violence of the mob.

36 For the multitude of the people followed after, crying out, "Away with him!"

37 And as Paul was about to be led into the barracks, he said to the commander, "May I speak to you?" He replied, "Can you speak Greek?

38 "Are you not the Egyptian who some time ago raised an insurrection and led the four thousand assassins out into the wilderness?"

39 But Paul said, "I am a Jew from Tarsus, in Cilicia, a citizen of no mean city; and I implore you, permit me to speak to the people."

40 So when he had given him permission, Paul stood on the stairs and motioned with his hand to the people. And when there was a great silence, he spoke to *them* in the Hebrew language, saying,

ACTS 22

"Men, brethren, and fathers, hear my defense before you now."

2 And when they heard that he spoke to them in the Hebrew language, they kept all the more silent. Then he said:

3 "I am indeed a Jew, born in Tarsus of Cilicia, but brought up in this city at the feet of Gamaliel, taught according to the strictness of our fathers' law, and was zealous toward God as you all are today.

4 "I persecuted this Way to the death, binding and delivering into prisons both men and women,

5 "as also the high priest bears me witness, and all the council of the elders, from whom I also received letters to the brethren, and went to Damascus to bring in chains even those who were there to Jerusalem to be punished.

6 "Now it happened, as I journeyed and came near Damascus at about noon, suddenly a great light from heaven shone around me.

7 "And I fell to the ground and heard a voice saying to me, 'Saul, Saul, why are you persecuting Me?'

8 "So I answered, 'Who are You, Lord?' And He said to me, 'I am Jesus of Nazareth, whom you are persecuting.'

9 "Now those who were with me indeed saw the light and were afraid, but they did not hear the voice of Him who spoke to me.

10 "So I said, 'What shall I do, Lord?' And the Lord said to me, 'Arise and go into Damascus, and there you will be told all things which are appointed for you to do.'

11 "And since I could not see for the glory of that light, being led by the hand of those who were with me, I came into Damascus.

12 "Then one, Ananias, a devout man according to the law, having a good testimony with all the Jews who dwelt *there,*

13 "came to me; and he stood and said to me, 'Brother Saul, receive your sight.' And at that same hour I looked up at him.

14 "Then he said, 'The God of our fathers has chosen you that you should know His will, and see the Just One, and hear the voice of His mouth.

15 'For you will be His witness to all men of what you have seen and heard.

16 'And now why are you waiting? Arise and be baptized, and wash away your sins, calling on the name of the Lord.'

17 "Then it happened, when I returned to Jerusalem and was praying in the temple, that I was in a trance

18 "and saw Him saying to me, 'Make haste and get out of Jerusalem quickly, for they will not receive your testimony concerning Me.'

19 "So I said, 'Lord, they know that in every synagogue I imprisoned and beat those who believe on You.

20 'And when the blood of Your martyr Stephen was shed, I also was standing by consenting to his death, and guarding the clothes of those who were killing him.'

21 "Then He said to me, 'Depart, for I will send you far from here to the Gentiles.'"

22 And they listened to him until this word, and *then* they raised their voices and said, "Away with such a *fellow* from the earth, for he is not fit to live!"

23 Then, as they cried out and tore off *their* clothes and threw dust into the air,

24 the commander ordered him to be brought into the barracks, and said that he should be examined under scourging, so that he might know why they shouted so against him.

25 And as they bound him with thongs, Paul said to the centurion who stood by, "Is it lawful for you to scourge a man who is a Roman, and uncondemned?"

26 When the centurion heard *that,* he went and told the commander, saying, "Take care what you do, for this man is a Roman."

27 Then the commander came and said to him, "Tell me, are you a Roman?" He said, "Yes."

28 And the commander answered, "With a large sum I obtained this citizenship." And Paul said, "But I was born *a citizen.*"

29 Then immediately those who were about to examine him withdrew from him; and the commander was also afraid after he found out that he was a Roman, and because he had bound him.

30 The next day, because he wanted to know for certain why he was accused by the Jews, he released him from *his* bonds, and commanded the chief priests

and all their council to appear, and brought Paul down and set him before them.

ACTS 23

Then Paul, looking earnestly at the council, said, "Men *and* brethren, I have lived in all good conscience before God until this day."

2 And the high priest Ananias commanded those who stood by him to strike him on the mouth.

3 Then Paul said to him, "God will strike you, *you* whitewashed wall! For you sit to judge me according to the law, and do you command me to be struck contrary to the law?"

4 And those who stood by said, "Do you revile God's high priest?"

5 Then Paul said, "I did not know, brethren, that he was the high priest; for it is written, '*You shall not speak evil of the ruler of your people.*' "

6 But when Paul perceived that one part were Sadducees and the other Pharisees, he cried out in the council, "Men *and* brethren, I am a Pharisee, the son of a Pharisee; concerning the hope and resurrection of the dead I am being judged!"

7 And when he had said this, a dissension arose between the Pharisees and the Sadducees; and the assembly was divided.

8 For *the* Sadducees say that there is no resurrection — and no angel or spirit; but the Pharisees confess both.

9 Then there arose a loud outcry. And the scribes *who were* of the Pharisees' party arose and protested, saying, "We find no evil in this man; but if a spirit or an angel has spoken to him, let us not fight against God."

10 And when there arose a great dissension, the commander, fearing lest Paul might be pulled to pieces by them, commanded the soldiers to go down and take him by force from among them, and bring *him* into the barracks.

11 But the following night the Lord stood by him and said, "Be of good cheer, Paul; for as you have testified for Me in Jerusalem, so you must also bear witness at Rome."

12 And when it was day, some of the Jews banded together and bound themselves under an oath, saying that they would neither eat nor drink till they had killed Paul.

13 Now there were more than forty who had formed this conspiracy.

14 They came to the chief priests and elders, and said, "We have bound ourselves under a great oath that we will eat nothing until we have killed Paul.

15 "Now you, therefore, together with the council, suggest to the commander that he be brought down to you tomorrow, as though you were going to make further inquiries concerning him; but we are ready to kill him before he comes near."

16 And when Paul's sister's son heard of their ambush, he went and entered the barracks and told Paul.

17 Then Paul called one of the centurions to *him* and said, "Take this young man to the commander, for he has something to tell him."

18 So he took him and brought *him* to the commander and said, "Paul the prisoner called me to *him* and asked *me* to bring this young man to you. He has something to say to you."

19 Then the commander took him by the hand, went aside and asked *him* privately, "What is it that you have to tell me?"

20 And he said, "The Jews have agreed to ask that you bring Paul down to the council tomorrow, as though they were going to inquire more fully about him.

21 "But do not yield to them, for more than forty of them lie in wait for him, men who have bound themselves by an oath that they will neither eat nor drink till they have killed him; and now they are ready, waiting for the promise from you."

22 So the commander let the young man depart, and commanded *him,* "Tell no one that you have revealed these things to me."

23 And he called for two centurions, saying, "Prepare two hundred soldiers, seventy horsemen, and two hundred spearmen to go to Caesarea at the third hour of the night;

24 "and provide mounts to set Paul on, and bring *him* safely to Felix the governor."

25 He wrote a letter in the following manner:

26 "Claudius Lysias, to the most excellent governor Felix: Greetings.

27 "This man was seized by the Jews and was about to be killed by them. Coming with the troops I rescued him, having learned that he was a Roman.

28 "And when I wanted to know the reason they accused him, I brought him before their council.

29 "I found out that he was accused concerning questions of their law, but had nothing charged against him worthy of death or chains.

30 "And when it was told me that the Jews lay in wait for the man, I sent him immediately to you, and also commanded his accusers to state before you the charges against him. Farewell."

31 Then the soldiers, as they were commanded, took Paul and brought *him* by night to Antipatris.

32 The next day they left the horsemen to *go* on with him, and returned to the barracks.

33 When they came to Caesarea and had delivered the letter to the governor, they also presented Paul to him.

34 And when the governor had read *it,* he asked what province he was from. And when he understood that *he was* from Cilicia,

35 he said, "I will hear you when your accusers also have come." And he commanded him to be kept in Herod's Praetorium.

ACTS 24

Now after five days Ananias the high priest came down with the elders and a certain orator *named* Tertullus. These gave evidence to the governor against Paul.

2 And when he was called upon, Tertullus began his accusation, saying: "Seeing that through you we enjoy great peace, and prosperity is being brought to this nation by your foresight,

3 "we accept *it* always and in all places, most noble Felix, with all thankfulness.

4 "Nevertheless, not to be tedious to you any further, I beg you to hear, by your courtesy, a few words from us.

5 "For we have found this man *a* plague, a creator of dissension among all the Jews throughout the world, and a ringleader of the sect of the Nazarenes.

6 "He even tried to profane the temple, and we seized him, and wanted to judge him according to our law.

7 "But the commander Lysias came by and with great violence took *him* out of our hands,

8 "commanding his accusers to come to you. By examining him yourself you may ascertain all these things of which we accuse him."

9 And the Jews also assented, maintaining that these things were so.

10 Then Paul, after the governor had nodded to him to speak, answered: "Inasmuch as I know that you have been for many years a judge of this nation, I do the more cheerfully answer for myself,

11 "because you may ascertain that it is no more than twelve days since I went up to Jerusalem to worship.

12 "And they neither found me in the temple disputing with anyone nor inciting the crowd, either in the synagogues or in the city.

13 "Nor can they prove the things of which they now accuse me.

14 "But this I confess to you, that according to the Way which they call a sect, so I worship the God of my fathers, believing all things which are written in the Law and in the Prophets.

15 "I have hope in God, which they themselves also accept, that there will be a resurrection of *the* dead, both of *the* just and *the* unjust.

16 "This *being* so, I myself always strive to have a conscience without offense toward God and men.

17 "Now after many years I came to bring alms and offerings to my nation,

18 "in the midst of which some Jews from Asia found me purified in the temple, neither with a multitude nor with tumult.

19 "They ought to have been here before you to object if they had anything against me.

20 "Or else let those who are *here* themselves say if they found any wrongdoing in me while I stood before the council,

21 "unless *it is* for this one statement which I cried out, standing among them, 'Concerning the resurrection of the dead I am being judged by you this day.' "

22 But when Felix heard these things, having more accurate knowledge of *the* Way, he adjourned the proceedings and said, "When Lysias the commander comes down, I will make a decision on your case."

23 So he commanded the centurion to keep Paul and to let *him* have liberty, and told him not to forbid any of his friends to provide for or visit him.

24 And after some days, when Felix came with his wife Drusilla, who was Jewish, he sent for Paul and heard him concerning the faith in Christ.

25 Now as he reasoned about righteousness, self-control, and the judgment to come, Felix was afraid and answered, "Go away for now; when I have a convenient time I will call for you."

26 Meanwhile he also hoped that money would be given him by Paul, that he might release him. Therefore he sent for him more often and conversed with him.

27 But after two years Porcius Festus succeeded Felix; and Felix, wanting to do the Jews a favor, left Paul bound.

ACTS 25

Now when Festus had come to the province, after three days he went up from Caesarea to Jerusalem.

2 Then the high priest and the chief men of the Jews informed him against Paul; and they petitioned him,

3 asking a favor against him, that he would summon him to Jerusalem — while *they* lay in ambush along the road to kill him.

4 But Festus answered that Paul should be kept at Caesarea, and that he himself was going *there* shortly.

5 "Therefore," he said, "let those who have authority among you go down with *me* and accuse this man, to see if there is any fault in him."

6 And when he had remained among them more than ten days, he went down to Caesarea. And the next day, sitting on the judgment seat, he commanded Paul to be brought.

7 When he had come, the Jews who had come down from Jerusalem stood about and laid many serious complaints against Paul, which they could not prove,

8 while he answered for himself, "Neither against the law of the Jews, nor against the temple, nor against Caesar have I offended in anything at all."

9 But Festus, wanting to do the Jews a favor, answered Paul and said, "Are you willing to go up to Jerusalem and there be judged before me concerning these things?"

10 Then Paul said, "I stand at Caesar's judgment seat, where I ought to be judged. To the Jews I have done no wrong, as you very well know.

11 "For if I am an offender, or have committed

anything worthy of death, I do not object to dying; but if there is nothing in these things of which these men accuse me, no one can deliver me to them. I appeal to Caesar."

12 Then Festus, when he had conferred with the council, answered, "You have appealed to Caesar? To Caesar you shall go!"

13 And after some days King Agrippa and Bernice came to Caesarea to greet Festus.

14 When they had been there many days, Festus laid Paul's case before the king, saying: "There is a certain man left a prisoner by Felix,

15 "about whom the chief priests and the elders of the Jews informed *me,* when I was in Jerusalem, asking for a judgment against him.

16 "To them I answered, 'It is not the custom of the Romans to deliver any man to destruction before the accused meets the accusers face to face, and has opportunity to answer for himself concerning the charge against him.'

17 "Therefore when they had come together, without any delay, the next day I sat on the judgment seat and commanded the man to be brought in.

18 "When the accusers stood up, they brought no accusation against him of such things as I supposed,

19 "but had some questions against him about their own religion and about one, Jesus, who had died, whom Paul affirmed to be alive.

20 "And because I was uncertain of such questions, I asked whether he was willing to go to Jerusalem and there be judged concerning these matters.

21 "But when Paul appealed to be reserved for the decision of Augustus, I commanded him to be kept till I could send him to Caesar."

22 Then Agrippa said to Festus, "I also would like to hear the man myself." "Tomorrow," he said, "you shall hear him."

23 So the next day, when Agrippa and Bernice had come with great pomp, and had entered the audi-

torium with the commanders and the prominent men of the city, at Festus' command Paul was brought in.

24 And Festus said: "King Agrippa and all the men who are here present with us, you see this man about whom the whole assembly of the Jews petitioned me, both at Jerusalem and here, crying out that he was not fit to live any longer.

25 "But when I found that he had committed nothing worthy of death, and that he himself had appealed to Augustus, I decided to send him.

26 "I have nothing certain to write to my lord concerning him. Therefore I have brought him out before you, and especially before you, King Agrippa, so that after the examination has taken place I may have something to write.

27 "For it seems to me unreasonable to send a prisoner and not to specify the charges against him."

ACTS 26

Then Agrippa said to Paul, "You are permitted to speak for yourself." So Paul stretched out his hand and answered for himself:

2 "I think myself happy, King Agrippa, because today I shall answer for myself before you concerning all the things of which I am accused by the Jews,

3 "especially because you are expert in all customs and questions which have to do with the Jews. Therefore I beg you to hear me patiently.

4 "My manner of life from my youth, which was spent from the beginning among my own nation at Jerusalem, all the Jews know.

5 "They knew me from the first, if they were willing to testify, that according to the strictest sect of our religion I lived a Pharisee.

6 "And now I stand and am judged for the hope of the promise made by God to our fathers.

7 "To this *promise* our twelve tribes, earnestly serv-

ing *God* night and day, hope to attain. For this hope's sake, King Agrippa, I am accused by the Jews.

8 "Why should it be thought incredible by you that God raises the dead?

9 "Indeed, I myself thought I must do many things contrary to the name of Jesus of Nazareth.

10 "This I also did in Jerusalem, and many of the saints I shut up in prison, having received authority from the chief priests; and when they were put to death, I cast my vote against *them*.

11 "And I punished them often in every synagogue and compelled *them* to blaspheme; and being exceedingly enraged against them, I persecuted *them* even to foreign cities.

12 "While thus occupied, as I journeyed to Damascus with authority and commission from the chief priests,

13 "at midday, O king, along the road I saw a light from heaven, brighter than the sun, shining around me and those who journeyed with me.

14 "And when we all had fallen to the ground, I heard a voice speaking to me and saying in the Hebrew language, 'Saul, Saul, why are you persecuting Me? *It is* hard for you to kick against the goads.'

15 "So I said, 'Who are You, Lord?' And He said, 'I am Jesus, whom you are persecuting.

16 'But rise and stand on your feet; for I have appeared to you for this purpose, to make you a minister and a witness both of the things which you have seen and of the things which I will yet reveal to you.

17 'I will deliver you from the *Jewish* people, as well as *from* the Gentiles, to whom I now send you,

18 'to open their eyes and to turn *them* from darkness to light, and *from* the power of Satan to God, that they may receive forgiveness of sins and an inheritance among those who are sanctified by faith in Me.'

19 "Therefore, King Agrippa, I was not disobedient to the heavenly vision,

20 "but declared first to those in Damascus and in

Jerusalem, and throughout all the region of Judea, and *then* to the Gentiles, that they should repent, turn to God, and do works befitting repentance.

21 "For these reasons the Jews seized me in the temple and tried to kill *me*.

22 "Therefore, having obtained help from God, to this day I stand, witnessing both to small and great, saying no other things than those which the prophets and Moses said would come —

23 "that the Christ would suffer, that He would be the first to rise from the dead, and would proclaim light to the *Jewish* people and to the Gentiles."

24 Now as he thus made his defense, Festus said with a loud voice, "Paul, you are beside yourself! Much learning is driving you mad!"

25 But he said, "I am not mad, most noble Festus, but speak the words of truth and reason.

26 "For the king, before whom I also speak freely, knows these things; for I am convinced that none of these things escapes his attention, since this thing was not done in a corner.

27 "King Agrippa, do you believe the prophets? I know that you do believe."

28 Then Agrippa said to Paul, "You almost persuade me to become a Christian."

29 And Paul said, "I would to God that not only you, but also all who hear me today, might become both almost and altogether such as I am, except for these chains."

30 When he had said these things, the king stood up, as well as the governor and Bernice and those who sat with them;

31 and when they had gone aside, they talked among themselves, saying, "This man is doing nothing worthy of death or chains."

32 Then Agrippa said to Festus, "This man might have been set free if he had not appealed to Caesar."

ACTS 27

And when it was decided that we should sail to Italy, they delivered Paul and some other prisoners to *one* named Julius, a centurion of the Augustan Regiment.

2 So, entering a ship of Adramyttium, we put to sea, meaning to sail along the coasts of Asia. Aristarchus, a Macedonian of Thessalonica, was with us.

3 And the next *day* we landed at Sidon. And Julius treated Paul kindly and gave *him* liberty to go to his friends and receive care.

4 When we had put to sea from there, we sailed under *the shelter of* Cyprus, because the winds were contrary.

5 And when we had sailed over the sea which is off Cilicia and Pamphylia, we came to Myra, *a city* of Lycia.

6 There the centurion found an Alexandrian ship sailing to Italy, and he put us on board.

7 And when we had sailed slowly many days, and arrived with difficulty off Cnidus, the wind not permitting us to proceed, we sailed under *the shelter of* Crete off Salmone.

8 Passing it with difficulty, we came to a place called Fair Havens, near the city *of* Lasea.

9 Now when much time had been spent, and sailing was now dangerous because the Fast was already over, Paul advised them,

10 saying, "Men, I perceive that this voyage will end with disaster and much loss, not only of the cargo and ship, but also our lives."

11 Nevertheless the centurion was more persuaded by the helmsman and the owner of the ship than by the things spoken by Paul.

12 And because the harbor was not suitable to winter in, the majority advised to set sail from there also, if by any means they could reach Phoenix, a harbor of Crete opening toward the southwest and northwest, *and* winter *there*.

13 When the south wind blew softly, supposing

that they had obtained *their* purpose, putting out to sea, they sailed close by Crete.

14 But not long after, a tempestuous head wind arose, called Euroclydon.

15 So when the ship was caught, and could not head into the wind, we let *her* drive.

16 And running under *the shelter of* an island called Clauda, we secured the skiff with difficulty.

17 When they had taken it on board, they used cables to undergird the ship; and fearing lest they should run aground on the Syrtis *Sands*, they struck sail and so were driven.

18 And because we were exceedingly tempest-tossed, the next *day* they lightened the ship.

19 On the third *day* we threw the ship's tackle overboard with our own hands.

20 Now when neither sun nor stars appeared for many days, and no small tempest beat on *us*, all hope that we would be saved was finally given up.

21 But after long abstinence from food, then Paul stood in the midst of them and said, "Men, you should have listened to me, and not have sailed from Crete and incurred this disaster and loss.

22 "And now I urge you to take heart, for there will be no loss of life among you, but only of the ship.

23 "For there stood by me this night an angel of the God to whom I belong and whom I serve,

24 "saying, 'Do not be afraid, Paul; you must be brought before Caesar; and indeed God has granted you all those who sail with you.'

25 "Therefore take heart, men, for I believe God that it will be just as it was told me.

26 "However, we must run aground on a certain island."

27 But when the fourteenth night had come, as we were driven up and down in the Adriatic *Sea*, about midnight the sailors sensed that they were drawing near some land.

28 And they took soundings and found *it* to be

twenty fathoms; and when they had gone a little farther, they took soundings again and found *it* to be fifteen fathoms.

29 Then, fearing lest we should run aground on the rocks, they dropped four anchors from the stern, and prayed for day to come.

30 And as the sailors were seeking to escape from the ship, when they had let down the skiff into the sea, under pretense of putting out anchors from the prow,

31 Paul said to the centurion and the soldiers, "Unless these men stay in the ship, you cannot be saved."

32 Then the soldiers cut away the ropes of the skiff and let it fall off.

33 And as day was about to dawn, Paul implored *them* all to take food, saying, "Today is the fourteenth day you have waited and continued without food, and eaten nothing.

34 "Therefore I urge you to take nourishment, for this is for your survival, since not a hair will fall from the head of any of you."

35 And when he had said these things, he took bread and gave thanks to God in the presence of them all; and when he had broken *it* he began to eat.

36 Then they were all encouraged, and also took food themselves.

37 And in all we were two hundred and seventy-six persons on the ship.

38 So when they had eaten enough, they lightened the ship and threw out the wheat into the sea.

39 Now when it was day, they did not recognize the land; but they observed a bay with a beach, onto which they planned to run the ship if possible.

40 And they let go the anchors and left *them* in the sea, meanwhile loosing the rudder ropes; and they hoisted the mainsail to the wind and made for shore.

41 But striking a place where two seas met, they ran the ship aground; and the prow stuck fast and remained immovable, but the stern was being broken up by the violence of the waves.

42 Now the soldiers' plan was to kill the prisoners, lest any of them should swim away and escape.

43 But the centurion, wanting to save Paul, kept them from *their* purpose, and commanded that those who could swim should jump *overboard* first and get to land,

44 and the rest, some on boards and some on *broken pieces* of the ship. And so it was that they all escaped safely to land.

ACTS 28

N ow when they had escaped, they then found out that the island was called Malta.

2 And the natives showed us unusual kindness; for they kindled a fire and made us all welcome, because of the rain that was falling and because of the cold.

3 But when Paul had gathered a bundle of sticks and laid *them* on the fire, a viper came out because of the heat, and fastened on his hand.

4 So when the natives saw the creature hanging from his hand, they said to one another, "No doubt this man is a murderer, whom, though he has escaped the sea, yet justice does not allow to live."

5 But he shook off the creature into the fire and suffered no harm.

6 However, they were expecting that he would swell up or suddenly fall down dead; but after they had looked for a long time and saw no harm come to him, they changed their minds and said that he was a god.

7 Now in that region there was an estate of the leading citizen of the island, whose name was Publius, who received us and entertained us courteously for three days.

8 And it happened that the father of Publius lay sickk of a fever and dysentery. Paul went in to him and prayed, and he laid his hands on him and healed him.

9 So when this was done, the rest of those on the

island who had diseases also came and were healed.

10 They also honored us in many ways; and when we departed, they provided such things as were necessary.

11 After three months we sailed in an Alexandrian ship whose figurehead was the Twin Brothers, which had wintered at the island.

12 And landing at Syracuse, we stayed three days.

13 From there we circled round and reached Rhegium. And after one day the south wind blew; and the next day we came to Puteoli,

14 where we found brethren, and were invited to stay with them seven days. And so we went toward Rome.

15 And from there, when the brethren heard about us, they came to meet us as far as Appii Forum and Three Inns. When Paul saw them, he thanked God and took courage.

16 Now when we came to Rome, the centurion delivered the prisoners to the captain of the guard; but Paul was permitted to dwell by himself with the soldier who guarded him.

17 And it came to pass after three days that Paul called the leaders of the Jews together. So when they had come together, he said to them: "Men *and* brethren, though I have done nothing against our people or the customs of our fathers, yet I was delivered as a prisoner from Jerusalem into the hands of the Romans,

18 "who, when they had examined me, wanted to let *me* go, because there was no cause for putting me to death.

19 "But when the Jews spoke against *it,* I was compelled to appeal to Caesar, not that I had anything of which to accuse my nation.

20 "For this reason therefore I have called for you, to see *you* and speak with *you,* because for the hope of Israel I am bound with this chain."

21 And they said to him, "We neither received

letters from Judea concerning you, nor have any of the brethren who came reported or spoken any evil of you.

22 "But we desire to hear from you what you think; for concerning this sect, we know that it is spoken against everywhere."

23 So when they had appointed him a day, many came to him at *his* lodging, to whom he explained and solemnly testified of the kingdom of God, persuading them concerning Jesus from both the Law of Moses and the Prophets, from morning till evening.

24 And some were persuaded by the things which were spoken, and some disbelieved.

25 So when they did not agree among themselves, they departed after Paul had said one word: "The Holy Spirit spoke rightly through Isaiah the prophet to our fathers,

26 "saying, 'Go to this people and say: "Hearing you will hear, and shall not understand; and seeing you will see, and not perceive;

27 "for the heart of this people has grown dull. Their ears are hard of hearing, and their eyes they have closed, lest they should see with *their* eyes and hear with *their* ears, *lest* they should understand with *their* heart and turn, so that I should heal them."'

28 "Therefore let it be known to you that the salvation of God has been sent to the Gentiles, and they will hear it!"

29 And when he had said these words, the Jews departed and had a great dispute among themselves.

30 Then Paul dwelt two whole years in his own rented house, and received all who came to him,

31 preaching the kingdom of God and teaching the things which concern the Lord Jesus Christ with all confidence, no one forbidding him.

⚏ LIVING WAY MINISTRIES

Reaching to Touch . . .
. . . Teaching to Change

Along with *Spirit-Filled,* three additional books are available in this series by Jack Hayford:

"Newborn: Alive In Christ, The Savior"

Expressly prepared for the new believer as a clear statement of exactly what Christ's salvation and one's new birth involve. A practical guide for learning to walk and live in the Family of God.

"Water Baptism: Sealed By Christ, The Lord"

A simple but profound handbook on the meaning and dynamic of water baptism. Written to the new believer, but designed so that even the most advanced will discover fuller dimensions of truth about their resources in Christ since their water baptism.

"Daybreak: Walking Daily In Christ's Presence"

Converts generalized exhortations about "daily devotions" into a workable, nonlegalistic set of specifics as to how the earnest believer can develop a fulfilling devotional prayer life. *Not* a devotional book; but a practical guide to the individual's own spiritual walk with Christ on a daily basis.

OTHER BOOKS BY JACK HAYFORD:

"Stepping Up in Faith"

A new call has gone out around the world — a call to believers to unite in concerts of prayer, joining in faith for spiritual breakthrough at a global dimension. In *Stepping Up In Faith,* Pastor Hayford takes us step by step along the pathway of prayer, showing us what Jesus taught about how to pray and how to live and grow in vital faith.

"Prayer Is Invading the Impossible"

Prayer is not the mystical experience of a few special people, but an aggressive act in the face of impossibility — an act that may be performed by anyone who will accept the challenge to learn to pray. Here is a practical "how-to" book that will get you started on the road to effective prayer (1977, Logos International and 1983, Ballantine Books).

"The Church On The Way"

How God taught the people of Van Nuys; how they discovered the pathway to worship, how prayer gatherings can be infused with lifegiving power, how genuine faith becomes active in intercession, and how God "ruined" a man's dream of his own future and gave him a vision of the Glory of the Lord.

Coming In This Series

"Breadbreaking: Feeding Daily on God's Word"

Here is a practical guide to your personal use of the Bible. An intended companion volume to *Daybreak* and *Partnership,* this book is designed to provide patterns for reading, studying, sharing, meditating upon and memorizing God's Word.

"Breakthrough: Joining With Jesus the Intercessor"

Intercessory prayer is as readily a part of the young believer's life as the seasoned saint's. The workability of a fulfilling and penetrating approach to deeper prayer is shown, as Pastor Hayford presents "The Other Side of the Prayer-Coin" begun in *Daybreak.*

AUDIO TAPES BY PASTOR HAYFORD

To complement and supplement your reading, audio cassette tapes of related teachings by Pastor Hayford are available through the SoundWord Tape Ministry. The following is a suggested list which correlates closely with the theme of *Spirit-Filled.*

TITLE	TAPE NUMBER
"How to Receive the Baptism with the Holy Spirit"	267
"Now that You Have Received the Baptism with the Holy Spirit"	1302
"The Great Psychiatrist: The Holy Spirit, I"	1374
"The Great Psychiatrist: The Holy Spirit, II"	1376
"Beginning with the Spiritual Gifts"	587

Please refer to the tape number when ordering.

These and other audio cassette tapes, as well as a complete catalog of tapes by Pastor Hayford, are available by writing to:

**SoundWord Tape Ministry
14300 Sherman Way
Van Nuys, CA 91405-2499**

VIDEOTAPES

For use in homes, Bible Studies, small group meetings and churches, videotapes may be special ordered. For information and a catalog of current listings, please write to:

**Living Way Ministries
14300 Sherman Way
Van Nuys, CA 91405-2499**